FATIMA
of
SINDH

CHACHA MOHAMMED ALI LAGHARI
Translated from Sindhi by MOHAN GEHANI

Lightning Fast Book Publishing, LLC

www.lfbookpublishing.com

All rights reserved. No part of this book may be reproduced or transmitted in any form or by any means—electronic, mechanical, photo- copying, recording, or otherwise—without written permission from the author, except for the inclusion of brief quotations in a review.

The author of this book offers a chronological account of his wife's life, and her impactful journey fighting for the people of the Pakistani province of Sindh. In the event that you use or enact any of the material in this book, the author and publisher assume no responsibility for your actions.

The publisher, Lightning Fast Book Publishing, assumes no responsibility for any content presented in this book.

Copyright © 2022 Sufi Laghari
All rights reserved.

ISBN: 979-8-9852917-7-3

Dedicated to Mirzadi

The epitome of courage and self-sacrifice

Table of Contents

Foreword vii

Introduction ix

Chapter 1: Fatima of Sindh in Washington, DC 1

Chapter 2: Memories: Village of Bakhsho Laghari 5

Chapter 3: Fatima's Childhood 21

Chapter 4: Efforts for Fatima's Engagement 25

Chapter 5: Our Marriage 29

Chapter 6: An Addition to the Family 35

Chapter 7: Trapped in a Feudal Setup 37

Chapter 8: Crisis after Crisis 43

Chapter 9: Education of Children 47

Chapter 10: From Bakhsho Laghari to Hyderabad 51

Chapter 11: Some Steps Toward Prosperity 57

Chapter 12: Brothers to be Married 59

Chapter 13: Ups and Downs of Life..65
Chapter 14: Father Afflicted with Cancer..69
Chapter 15: Stepping into Politics..71
Chapter 16: Fatima "The Sindhi Nationalist"................................75
Chapter 17: Gathering in Bhit Shah...87
Chapter 18: May 29th Women's Protest..91
Chapter 19: Anwar's Marriage..95
Chapter 20: Incident of Tando Bahawal.......................................97
Chapter 21: Sister-in-Law Mirzadi...99
Chapter 22: Old Mother..103
Chapter 23: Saleh Junejo...105
Chapter 24: Fatima's Attitude toward Activists.........................109
Chapter 25: Chachi of Sindh Falls Sick..115
Chapter 26: My Brother's Death...119
Chapter 27: To America for Fatima's Treatment........................123
Chapter 28: My Mother: Reflections by Munawar....................131
Chapter 29: Remembering My Mother by Anwar.....................137
About The Author..145

Foreword

The father of Dr. Anwar Laghari and Munawar Laghari has written a book about his wife, Fatima. I met her in Hyderabad on two or three occasions. Though she was from a small village and uneducated, she was more advanced in her thinking than many of the leading urban women. She was sincere, and she loved this soil. In my opinion, she was more of an institution than an individual. She had to face many mental, emotional, and physical challenges in life, and she faced them with fortitude and courage. She kept her sense of humor alive even in the grimmest of situations.

For a long time, she pined to see her exiled son Munawar in the United States; it was a tragedy that he could not call or go to meet him for years. I was happy to hear that eventually she did reach Washington, DC, and visited with her son. Alas! It was too late. Her last days spent with Munawar are his real asset. I wish she had more time to live where she could have been a source of great inspiration to many women.

I am grateful that I had an opportunity to meet the mothers of Mazhar Sidiqui, Salim Memon, and Munawar Laghari who have cherished their soil in their hearts.

Fatima was not only mother to Munawar but also a mother to us all. She was our guide and teacher. May God grant her eternal peace!

With Prayers,

Altaf Shaikh

Introduction

This memoir is written by *Chacha* (Uncle) Mohammed Ali Laghari who hailed from a small village where he was educated only through primary school. He, his father, and their entire family were landless tillers. They belonged to a tribal, clannish society rooted in traditional values, including a fierce loyalty to kinship. It was a ruthlessly patriarchal society too. In that society even the men had no voice of their own except through their clan leader, and the question of whether women deserved a voice did not arise. The very existence of women was subordinate to the male will.

It is in this context that Mohammed Ali Laghari writes about his wife, Fatima, and her tribulations, courage, and dedication. Her journey into a political movement speaks volumes about her enlightened spirit, boldness, and courage of conviction.

This book will also provide source material for a history of the Jiye Sindh Movement (Sindhi Nationalist Movement) whenever such a book is written. That a man and woman from a lower strata of society with very limited education but with robust common sense could play a significant role in the Sindhi Nationalist Movement is in itself quite a significant achievement. This is in contrast with the electoral politics of Sindh today where a handful of feudal lords have created fiefdoms and maintain dominion over their respective "territories." The Sindhi Nationalist Movement is rooted in the soil of Sindh, and the sons of the soil are the mainstay of this movement.

It is necessary to understand the underlying causes for the movement; its roots lie deep in history as well as in recent political developments in the subcontinent of India. At the outset it is necessary to emphasize that linguistic and cultural boundaries are made by nature, and the people inhabiting specific areas where these boundaries are shared constitute one people. Crosscurrents and outside influences do play their role, but the core is not affected; those influences, if they percolate at all, become part of the soil and historical psyche of a people. In a historical context, *Political* boundaries—unique from these natural linguistic and cultural boundaries—are merely shifting sands.

In accordance with this philosophy, the state of Pakistan is an unnatural state. It seeks to rely on religion alone as the preeminent binding force, instead of other deep-rooted factors like language, culture, or ethnicity. The very concept of placing religion at the core of the country's identity is belied by the fact that so many states that profess the same Islamic religion exist across the globe. The breakup of Pakistan and the emergence of Bangladesh as a separate nation shattered the myth that religion alone may unite a state.

It is no secret that British imperialism played a significant role in the creation of modern-day Pakistan; all facts in this regard have been well documented by Captain Sarila (Aide-de-camp) in his book *The Shadow*

Introduction

of the Great Game, which was written to the last viceroy, Lord Mountbatten and in *Facts are Facts* by Wali Khan. The creation of Pakistan was to pursue the centuries-long policy of Russian containment. When the Soviet Union (USSR) was established as a communist state, this policy attained great significance in the geopolitical equations that emerged after the Second World War. Geopolitical equations are always in a state of flux, due to the inherent dynamics that accompany power shifts. There are always points of convergence and contention between states, and it is negotiating through these contradictions that the foreign policy of any country is conducted on tactical and strategic planes.

This is the lens through which to view the creation of Pakistan: It was engineered as an imperialist calculation in the midst of the Cold War. Pakistan's *raison d'être* is a sense of insecurity that arises from the Hindu-majority India. Pakistan thus inevitably seeks military parity with India; however, given the relative size of Pakistan and its resources, it simply cannot afford this parity. This conundrum has led Pakistan to become a client state of the dominant world power, the United States of America. Pakistan became hinged to the United States for military supplies and aid in the aftermath of the Second World War and the subsequent Cold War with the USSR. This resulted in a bloated military establishment that was not necessary for a country the size of Pakistan; this overgrown sense of power has generated a temptation to justify itself by involvement in civil affairs, leading to military takeover and the many years of military rule in Pakistan. Even when—for the sake of optics—civilian rule is established, the actual power rests with the military. Pakistan cannot survive as a civilian state.

Pakistan as it exists suffers from another serious flaw: its skewed demographic composition. The population of one province, Punjab, outweighs the population of all other provinces put together. Even in the best of democratic periods, this imbalance is apt to tempt Punjab to treat the rest of the provinces as colonies to be exploited, and these populations are relegated to a secondary status. In addition, there are refugees who came from India bringing a desire for conquest and triumph. They were mostly settled in Sindh, and they expressed themselves as rulers with the indigenous Sindhi population as their subjects. This has resulted in social, economic, and political confrontations aided and fueled by the Military-Punjabi axis.

There is a basic, deep-rooted ideological contradiction between the "Idea" of Pakistan and the historical ethos of Sindh. Pakistan derives its mandate from the rigid and fundamental-sectarian interpretation of Islam. This dates back to the rule of Aurangzeb when all religious institutions were put under the control of orthodox Islamists. In Sindh, however, the structure of Islamic institutions continued in the hands of liberal Islamists who owed their allegiance to Dara Shikoh, who was at his core Sufi. This resulted in a continuation of Sufi ethos in Sindh, which stands for a very liberal interpretation of Islam, which was reinforced by great poets including Shah Abdul Lati and Sachal who followed them in that tradition. This understanding continues today in Sindh, evident even through instances of Hindu-Muslim amity in the beginning of this book itself. *It is not possible to contain the Sindhi-Sufi ethos, nurtured through centuries, in a straitjacket—the Idea of Pakistan.*

Yet another fact that needs to be taken into consideration: Sindh was an independent, sovereign state until 1843; it was the last state to be conquered and annexed by the British. In a sense, the concept of being an independent, sovereign state is still alive in the minds of people in Sindh.

Introduction

The present Sindhi Nationalist Movement may be understood in this context. It was a great son of Sindh, Saeen G. M. Sayed, who shared a vision of Sindh freed from the bondage of Pakistan; he inspired many with his vision, especially young students as well as all poor and disposed people of Sindh. Many young lives and careers have been sacrificed to achieve this vision, which is opposed in Sindh only by those who are aligned with the existing political establishment. Pakistan, as stated earlier, has remained controlled by a virtual military dictatorship and as such, all channels of communication between ruler and ruled are absent; the ruler must thus rely on a number of spy agencies to gather information. The ruling elite's tendency to keep an eye on the activities of all sides contributes to the multiplicity of spy agencies. In this context, many leaders and cadre of the movement have unwittingly fallen to the machinations of those spy agencies, which successfully decimated the nationalist movement by engineering split after split from within. After the demise of Saaen G. M. Sayed, no towering personality has emerged to forge unity among various factions of the movement. It is in fact a Catch-22, where the absence of a clear mass movement leads to splintered groups, and without unity a true mass movement cannot be built.

It is self-evident that the Sindhi Nationalist Movement today is splintered and ebbing. That said, there are always periods of ebb and tide in any movement. What is the future of this movement? When does this ebbing period end and the tide rise again?

A strange quirk in geopolitical equations now finds Pakistan, a longtime ally of the United States, with abundant Chinese presence on its soil by virtue of China's Belt and Road Initiative. Thus, it can be said that Pakistan is riding two horses at the same time. The United States, for its strategic interest in Pakistan given the country's proximity to Afghanistan and ability to balance power in the region, cannot jettison its role at the present juncture and must actively contend with the presence of China, which has become a formidable rival in the political and economic spheres. There is, too, a discernible race between these two powers where artificial intelligence is concerned. As the potential for confrontation between these two powers looms increasingly large, the position in which Pakistan finds itself becomes unenviable. The "comfort" of riding two horses at once is likely to fall at any moment.

An idea never dies. It may be submerged for a time but when the tide turns, the idea may resurface with more vigor. In the grand scheme of a nation's history, a century or so does not ultimately hold much significance. Its effect remains only skin-deep. Saeen G. M. Sayed's vision may return with full force. It will have to work out new forms of struggle and adopt new strategies. It may have to wrap itself in a new idiom suited to the space-age and the era of artificial intelligence. It has been stated that, in space travel, the earth will forever remain the reference point for humans to find their bearings. Earth has been divided by nature in various linguistic zones, and language as the oldest tradition of humanity will connect humans like an umbilical cord to Mother Earth. In such a situation, language assumes a primal position. Linguistic identity forms part of any person's core, and in this vein it is certain that Sindh is bound to find its freedom from the State of Pakistan, which is rooted in a bigoted interpretation of Islam. Sufi philosophy contains a vision for a future of humanity in sync with the space-age, wherein every atom is connected through a divine spark. A bright future awaits humanity and my soil of Sindh.

- Introduction in English by **Mohan Gehani.**

Chapter 1

Fatima of Sindh in Washington, DC

Pining for my country if I die here
Soomra!* Send my body to my Panwhars*
May I breathe the fragrance of creepers of my forefathers
I will feel alive even when I am dead

— Shah Latif

Fatima and I were greeted by our son, Munawar, at the airport in Washington, DC, on May 1, 2008. He embraced his mother and saw that she was comfortably seated in the car. This gesture brought a glow of happiness to his sick mother's face as she was seeing her exiled son for the first time in 15 years. Hers was like the face of a mother seeing her newborn baby for the first time—among the most joyous moments in any life!

We passed skyscrapers and shops filled with all types of merchandise as we navigated the wide streets. Munawar aimed to keep his mother's spirits up and insisted that they could stop anywhere should she desire anything. "By seeing you I now have everything that I wanted in life, and now I have no desire to have anything else," she replied. Munawar called his friends and his world-famous Sister Dianna Ortiz as we reached home. Sister Dianna Ortiz was working for persecuted and oppressed people. They were told about Fatima's medical condition, and soon she was admitted to a secure hospital in Washington, DC.

The doctors were very courteous and helpful, but we were completely disappointed by the test results. Her cancer was at the last stage; it had spread throughout her entire body. Doctors insisted that, at that advanced stage, treatment was not possible. Doctor Shyamlal, who was practicing in Virginia, called Munawar the next day asking that we bring Fatima to him. We went, but his findings were the same as those of the previous hospital. All the doctors were unanimous in declaring that, at that stage, nothing could be done.

Fatima was not educated in any school, but she had learned valuable lessons as if by heart; *life* had been her teacher, exposing her to many difficulties and a few moments of innocent enjoyment. Though she could not understand a word of English, she could read everything from the facial expressions of the doctors and understood that her days were numbered. Munawar was adamant that in this most advanced country of the world, there *must* be some hospital where his mother could be treated and cured. Shah Latif has truly said: "Medicines can only help when mercy is bestowed."

While returning from Virginia, Fatima held Munawar's face in her hands, kissed him, and said: "For the last eighteen years, I have constantly longed to see you. Now my wish is fulfilled. Now allow me to go back to my

Chapter 1: Fatima of Sindh in Washington, DC

own country and my own people." Munawar was insistent and would not budge, arguing that she had just seen him after such a long time and that it was now his duty to serve her and find a doctor who could cure her. She simply whispered that her last wish, which was to see Munawar, had been fulfilled and that she would like to go back to her own soil and people. After a month's stay, it was decided that we would return to Sindh. All this time, my heart was wrenched. I was in a pensive mood and distraught in the Washington, DC airport, for the time of final parting with our son had come.

When we sat in the plane, Fatima's face clearly showed signs of satisfaction. "Mohammed Ali," she said, "the separation from Munawar for the last eighteen years has neither allowed me to live nor die. All this time I have spent in agony, as if sleeping on the pile of burning coals. Now I will die a peaceful death."

Hearing all this, my heart was rent apart. "Fatima," I said in a muffled cry, "how can you leave me like that? We have been together through all the ups and downs of life. We have shared food together for years. We have worked together in fields so that our children may have a good education."

"Now I am tired," she whispered. Tears flowed from my eyes and wet my cheeks. I could not control myself. The flood of memories rushed through my mind. With moist eyes, I could visualize each moment of our lives through my imagination.

Chapter 2

Memories: Village of Bakhsho Laghari

Our village, Bakhsho Laghari, is situated 21 kilometers east of Hyderabad. Elders would tell us that Bakhsho Laghari had existed for roughly one thousand years and that the village school had stood strong for more than one hundred years. The latter fact was verified by the records maintained at the school.

This village consists of about one hundred households inhabited by people from many clans, including people of African descent (Sheedis), Kalohara blacksmiths, Bhil tribals, fishermen, and even Sayeds. The village inhabitants are known by the names of their ancestors, regardless of clan; all Lagharis, for example, belong to the same clan but are differentiated by the name of their specific ancestors, thus maintaining a distinct identity. Among the Laghari clan are the Lalnis, Muzranis, Ghanoranis, Jiandanis and Juranis. There are no restrictions on intermarriages and inter-relationships between them. Our family is recognized from the view of the neighborhood as Ghanoranis. We have inherited this identity from our ancestors, and our name has become associated with hospitality, good behavior, humor, and tolerance. This is one the reasons that we can face the ups and downs of life with stoicism.

Bakhsho Laghari is a rural village, which subsists on agriculture and animal husbandry reflective of the broader Sindh province; more than 80 percent of the Sindhi population is engaged in these practices. Despite reliance on these industries, it was not until the fourth decade of the last century that there was a reliable irrigation system in place. Instead, most villages depended on local wells and waterwheels to water their fields, drinking and household purposes. Poor folk would busy themselves collecting water on the backs of their camels or mules when the water table would rise to fill the well, and they would at the same time get busy procuring the seed for their fields. They would engage in this backbreaking physical labor each day of the season, from sowing the fields to harvesting. They remained idle during the off-season, without productive activity, and thus needed to work hard to accumulate income for the whole year when they could.

Poor people were at high-risk for experiencing many health problems, and there was no hospital nearby; even roads were conspicuously absent. When in need of medical treatment, they would depend on the "miraculous" treatment of holy water and talismans of some holy Mulla or Pir. My father used to say that poor folk were illiterate and thus did not remember the exact years of their births and deaths. He recalled that when the eldest of his five brothers was about seven or eight years old, a plague ravaged the entire region, and thousands of people died in the city of Thatta. In Bakhsho Laghari, there seemed to be a new grave dug as soon as one burial was completed. It is said that all the people in the area where the Masudanis resided fell victim to the epidemic; in that family, only a brother and sister survived. It was during this period that my grandfather

Chapter 2: Memories: Village of Bakhsho Laghari

and his three brothers perished. Our grandmother, whose name incidentally, was also Fatima, had to shoulder the responsibility of bringing her children up alone; she would do the manual work necessary, and her elder brother helped her. This was the context of grim poverty in which they were raised. Two of my father's brothers would go to people's fields to graze animals to earn something, and gradually they began to work as laborers in the fields. The eldest brother was eventually married, and their mother passed away soon thereafter. She was a brave woman indeed! She had seen her husband and her three brothers-in-law succumb to the plague, leaving her alone to bring up her five sons ranging from the age of six months to seven years. Years later, she left for her heavenly abode; may her soul rest in peace!

Father used to tell us that, while he had not seen the different countries of the world, as an orphan he had led a life of deprivation steeped in poverty and disease. That experience of toil and hardship had imbued him and his brothers with a sense of humility and empathy, and they were always ready to lend a helping hand to anyone in need. If they were told to do any work for anyone, they never demurred or avoided it. They would not only contribute physically to render any sort of help but they also would at times bear a financial loss as well. This brought them recognition that was beyond any measure, which added not only to their personality but improved the position of our clan. We would be offered employment due our reputation, and we were well-compensated by shopkeepers.

At night in the village, we would hear the sounds of moving bullock carts, cries of camels moving through, and the twittering of birds. Every morning everyone would go to Gehimal's food grain and grocery shop, where deliveries from Hoosri station or Tando Alam Mari would arrive at the shops of Thakumal, Cholomal or Jethomal.

The main market, which consisted of about 20 shops, ran from north to south in the village. There were no tea shops at that time, for that practice came only after the establishment of Pakistan, and all shopkeepers were Hindus. Times have changed, though. In those days, food, milk, and milk products were available at home, and milk was never sold. It was a common saying that "sons and milk are not sold." Milk is, however, sold today, though sons are not for sale.

Two tailors were Brahmins who, apart from there vocation, would perform religious rituals on holy occasions for Hindus. They would conduct marriage and death rituals for Hindus, provide home remedies for illness, as well as worship their gods in Temples situated inside their homes. In the center of the village was one shop run by Mrs. Kimat, who would sell various kinds of pickles with such flavor that people my age still relish the taste, unable to forget it; I have wandered the length and breadth of Sindh, and never consumed such pickles again. The taste of Shikarpur pickles simply cannot compare. The same woman made delicious *Pakoras* too; by comparison those made by Kaloo near Hyder Chowk in the present day taste like mud.

Poor Muslim women at the time would work with men to harvest millet and wheat, make ghee from the curd, and make blankets out of cut piece cloth to generate income, which would be necessary when their daughters were married. Hindu women also played a role in running businesses in various ways. Our house was situated at the far end of southern edge of the village. When leaving for school each morning, I would grab a handful of grain, which I would sell at Uncle Thakumal's shop in exchange for two pennies, and during recess I would purchase chickpeas from Uncle Cholumal's shop. Uncle Cholumal was a loving person of a happy disposition, and his behavior with elders as well as children was endearing. He was a poor man, and his family depended on the sale of the chickpeas. Despite having no alternative source of income, he was no miser. He was a big-hearted man indeed! He would place cooked chickpeas on a large plate to sell in the village streets, and would arrive at school for recess each day. He would stand on a school bench at times as a joke, pretending to scold children so that they purchased his chickpeas; he would raise a bench from one end, and children would pretend to be afraid, leading to peals of laughter all around. If any child who did not have money to buy chickpeas from him was left standing alone in one corner, he would call to them and say, "It does not matter if you do not have money today. Have chickpeas today, and you may pay me tomorrow." That tomorrow would never come. I was one of the students who, experiencing poverty, had opportunities to eat chickpeas without ever paying him anything. I do not know where Uncle Cholumal is now, whether he is alive or dead; I am now in a position to pay him back, but there is no one to whom I can give and redeem this debt.

In the eastern side of the village, apart from main market, there was a lane of shops that ran parallel to each other; this was where all the workmen—the blacksmith, barber, carpenter, potter, brick-maker, and the like—resided. The potter, Ahmed, was a courageous and a heavy built man. He would have made a good wrestler, but he kept to his family tradition and became a potter. He had a kiln near his shop; there he would put a chunk of wet mud on the wheel and begin moving it while patting the mud to make it thin. When asked why he continued to pat the mud, he would explain that, if the pottery were not patted properly and made thin, the pots would be very thick and heavy. Then just as it takes two people to lift a heavy person, it would take two people to pick up his work. Patting the vessel makes it strong. He would then raise his finger and say philosophically, "I am a simple, small potter, but The Potter (God), when he pats a man and makes him strong, creates in him tolerance, patience, and courage with which he is able to face any difficulty in life …. When Sohini entered the furious river," he would continue, "her pitcher was neither properly baked nor strong. If she had carried a properly baked and strong pitcher, she would have not drowned in the river."

Ahmed the potter was also a very famous bonesetter in those days. This was once a traditional responsibility of potters and the washer man of the Soomra tribe who would grind a special semisolid earth to make a paste. This paste would be covered by a muslin cloth to create a mold— much like today's plaster casts, and the bone would soon be set. No one ever noticed any failure in Ahmed's bone setting. He was not only an expert bonesetter and potter, but a wise man whose advice in any matter would be sound. He was a prankster too.

Until the fourth decade of the last century, village workmen would not charge any money for their services; instead, at harvesttime, they would be given about 40 kilograms of grain from every field to make their living. This was sufficient for their sustenance. When Ahmed the potter once set out to retrieve his annual portion of harvested grain from one landlord, the landlord told him that the yield had been low, and that Ahmed would need to wait until the next year to claim his share. Ahmed immediately tied the hands of the landlord and measured his due share of the grain, telling the landlord that he had not taken a grain more than what was due to him. He then approached the chief of the village and told him about the entire incident. He asked the village chief to send someone to untie the landlord's hands and asserted that if the landlord had died of starvation because his hands were tied, he should not have been held responsible. For many days thereafter the landlord was ridiculed, and this incident continued to be a topic of village gossip. That landlord did not venture outside his walls for more than two months because he was ashamed.

On another occasion Ahmed the potter was mounting his donkey on the edge of a canal when a watchman, summoning all the authority of a government servant, rudely asked him if he did not know that riding a donkey on the edge of canal was prohibited. He ordered Ahmed to dismount his steed. Ahmed the potter requested that he be allowed to ride his donkey in this instance, given that the surrounding area was planted with thorns. The watchman did not relent. This infuriated Ahmed the potter, who immediately tied the watchman hand and foot, put him on the donkey, and brought him to Chief Adam Khan. Upon hearing and seeing a growing crowd of curious onlookers, the chief came out to ask what the matter was. Ahmed the potter humbly narrated the entire incident to him. The chief requested that, as a government servant, the watchman should be untied and honorably placed on the cot alongside his fellow servants where he would be allowed to share his version of the incident.

The village barbers, apart from plying their normal trade, were employed as cooks during marriages and death ceremonies and as able healers for any boils or wounds with their specially made ointments. They would also remove the foreskin of Muslim boys when they came of age. Juma the barber was fondly called "Sagrou" by villagers. Nawaz Ali, though belonging to that community, was considered as a pious man; his brothers and cousins carried on their ancestral work, but he never held scissors of blade in his hands. He would often pick a harmonium and sing Sufi songs that would touch the heart. He was good at singing "Tilang Raga," but at night when he sang "Rano Raga," it seemed that the entire existence had come to a standstill to hear his melody. His rendering of Misri

Shah's verses, in particular, would transport one into a spiritual world. His music would demolish all walls and the distinctions of religions and hatred. He never sang for money and never asked anyone for anything. He was so humble that he would move about with his eyes cast down and away from the gossip of the world; he was respected by all—the poor as well as the rich. Seeing him, one was reminded of this line from Shah Latif's verse:

> *He does not ask of caste or position*
> *Only who works hard, only gets successes.*

I believe that he was a hidden gem. Due to his humble disposition and poor condition, he could not receive wider recognition. His elder brother Soomar Faqir was a worldly man. Nawaz Ali continued with his traditional work and this way, they eked out their living. Soomar, apart from his traditional work, would remove the spots of horses and mend the shoulders of bullocks.

Two carpentry workshops, which doubled as family homes were situated on the eastern side of the village. The larger shop belonged to Manomal and his son Lalumal. Manomal made cots that would last for decades. Weary travelers would often tie their donkeys and horses outside their home and wait for a while at their shop to get the news of happenings in the region as well as distant places. Even landlords would dismount from their horses to visit this place and exchange tidings. This was how information and news were disseminated in the age before newspapers and televisions. In those times, good wood was used, and proper workmanship was done. There was no need to rush about the work and do an inferior or shoddy job as is the practice now. The houses that Manomal and Lalumal built still remain in the village. Their descendants continue with the same work, and now they are doing quite well for themselves with 20 acres of land.

Opposite them were houses of the village blacksmiths, Ali Mohammed and Haroon. They made very sharp and durable cutting instruments, which would cut through any dense material with ease. Though Ali Mohammed was merely a blacksmith, his wise words were remembered by the people of many villages spread across miles. He was an entertainer and amusing person whose company was craved by young and old, rich and poor alike. I have seen many reputable people meeting him with due respect.

In the eastern lane itself were houses of traditional musicians, the Manganhars. They would play musical instruments at the accompaniment of a traditional drum, Dhol, and they would create a festive atmosphere with traditional marriage songs. The satisfaction or joy conveyed by film music, which blares from loudspeakers at today's wedding ceremonies cannot compare to this ancient craft. If any marriage took place without the Manganhars' presence, attendees would mistake it for an occasion of mourning rather than the happy occasion it was meant to be. This traditional tribe of musicians would invoke divine blessings for the couple and the entire family. For seven days before a marriage, the bride was kept confined; a number of rituals and ceremonies would be conducted in her confinement, and musicians would play mornings and evenings for all seven days. Musicians were paid handsomely so that they would be able to make a modest living, and they were given grains from fields of the surrounding villages.

In the fourth decade of the last century, cars and buses were unheard of in interior Sindh. It was common for anyone with means to own a mare or a horse. The musicians would teach infant animals to walk, a complicated art, which was done over various stages. A proper steed would be judged by its speed as well as the extent to which a rider did not feel any sudden jerk in spite of the horse's speed. To test the latter, a rider would hold a cup filled with clarified butter in his hand while riding; a passing mark meant that not a drop could spill. Horse owners would organize competitions for their horses and riders to test this skill. In races today, a galloping horse may be valued at millions of dollars, but such was not the case in interior Sindh. The following saying was common in those days: "Sons and horses who are stubborn are the most beloved."

The homes in the southern side of the village belonged to scavengers, and that continues to be true today. Two homes had shops situated in front of them—the homes of Foto and Kacho. Foto was an expert in making ladies footwear, and Kacho was a tanner and an expert in making decorative objects to place upon horses—objects that he would mend and polish as well. His expertise inspired such an awe that even a wealthy person would not come before him without leaving his footwear outside. Foto and Kacho were above religion and were Sufis in their outlook. In the morning, after having a bath, they would sing Sufi songs on one-stringed instruments. The songs of Mohammed Fakir were popular with them. Their voices had a quality that would attract people toward them, and many would gather to hear them sing with joyful abandon. Their songs would melt all the feelings of differences and hatred. The individuals in their audience would become bound with an invisible thread of unity, as if they were one, regardless of wealth or creed. As Sachal said:

"I am neither a Muslim nor Hindu

I am what I am."

Chapter 2: Memories: Village of Bakhsho Laghari

Just as trees and plants are washed from dirt with rainfall, their songs would make the hearts of listeners fresh and free from any dirt (i.e., malice), which may have accumulated over time. They would often be invited by Muslim landlords to sing at their public places and by Hindu businessmen to sing at their open business places. They never made it their profession. It was all out of love, to spread a deeply spiritual message that all are united. My father would sometimes invite them. They had earned that trust, respect, and goodwill, which is a wealth in itself, through their good behavior and ethical living practices. I believe that in comparison to any extremist Mullas, these faqeers (mystics) would be enjoying their afterlife in heaven.

Such was the atmosphere of unity and harmony in my village, Bakhsho Laghari, and its vicinity. This place never witnessed any communal strife between the two different religious communities nor did it witness any distinctions between the Shia and Sunni Muslim sects. Followers of both sects continued to offer Friday prayers in the common mosque. All festivals such as Eid, Holi, and Diwali were celebrated together. During the Holi festival, Uncle Cholumal and the shop owner, Seth Gehimal, would carry a bucket full of paint and drench every passerby, be they Hindu or Muslim. All were happy, and the atmosphere of mirth and merriment prevailed. Hindus celebrating Diwali would distribute sweetmeat throughout the village, and the earthen lamps lit with pure ghee in their shops and houses would convert the village into a fairyland. I would take five pies or some grain from home and purchase sweets from Tahkumal's shop. During Eid, Muslims would share "Sewaain" with everyone, and even Hindus would embrace Muslims and exchange proper greetings after Eid prayers.

Fatima's and my parents were poor. My father, Gulan Khan, and his brother Hassan Ali worked as manual laborers at the construction site of the Sukkur barrage for four annas a day, or about one-fourth of a rupee. As a child I would ask my father about the marks that I saw on his shoulder when he would remove his shirt. He would reply that, after digging holes deep enough, they would throw the heavy bags on the top of the embankments. He toiled twelve hours a day every day of the week to make a living for his family.

Fatima lost her father when she was four or five years of age. Her mother worked hard to raise her along with three sons. She was a self-respecting person who did not crave anyone's sympathy; instead, she relied on her own work ethic. She sent her son, Ahmed Ali, to school at the age of seven. She would make blankets from rags, curd, and clarified butter from milk and then sell those products in the local market. She worked as a laborer in the fields at harvesttime—all to make a modest living for her family. The burden of the household work fell on Fatima's shoulders at the tender age of five. Our houses were separated by only one lane, but I never saw Fatima playing with her mates at any time of day. She would carry her infant brother Shoutkat on her shoulder and drag her three-year-old brother by his arm to go buy groceries from Uncle Thakumai's shop. Fatima would also help sell the blankets made from rags and other garments embroidered by her mother.

It has remained a tradition in our society to give preference to sons, not daughters. This tradition has not at its core evolved, even in the twenty-first century, although it was certainly more pronounced in the middle of the last century. Today, more often than not, the good food, clothes, and education are reserved for the boys of the household. It is perceived that a girl's value is destined to be transferred to another family, and this

Chapter 2: Memories: Village of Bakhsho Laghari

vein discrimination on the basis of gender continues to this day. Men are considered the incarnation of God upon earth, which means that it is the duty—and at times a matter of pride—for wives to obey the husband's every whim and order. This distinction between genders was negligible in our village, which was steeped in Sufi tradition. The men and women of poor families would work well together in the fields. It was very rare that one would hear about domestic violence against women. Girls of the village were highly respected by all villagers. In normal life there was not much difference between poor or Hindu and Muslim communities. If any issue arose, both would sit together to arrive at an amicable solution, and Master Moolchand would often be called to arbitrate.

It did not matter in our village whether a family was wealthy; there was not much pomp and show in those days, and decency was valued above all else. For example, the rich landlord Rais Bhadur Khan wed his daughter to Fatima's uncle even though he belonged to a poor family. My father used to tell us that his own marriage was arranged with the help of the family of a rich landlord, Rais Adam Khan, and was solemnized on August 7, 1940. The Ghanorais were our neighbors, and because they were very witty and full of humor, they were much sought after as company at village gatherings. The Lalanis were very secure financially and hosted well-decorated gatherings. That said, our place was best for common gatherings, and we would host afternoon gatherings in our home, after everyone was free of the day's routine; Rais Adam Khan, the Lalanis, and many others would attend. The hookah would always be fresh, and many would puff it one after another. News from many places would be exchanged at our gatherings, and someone would always express valuable commentary or crack a joke, which would send everyone into peals of laughter.

In the south of the village, beyond the pit, there were houses that belonged to five or more families of people of African descent. They were quite hardy and very hardworking. Their ancestors must have been captured in some war and sold as slaves at some point in the past, for them to have arrived there. They continued to be sold as slaves from the time of the Arabs until the time of the Talpur Mirs dynasty. There has been no slavery since the advent of British rule, but hunger, dire poverty, and ignorance have continued to plague their descendants.

There were two wells on the eastern side of the village, both constructed by some philanthropic Hindu. Men and women of Hindu and Muslim backgrounds would fetch water at the well without distinction. Water from the wells would, surprisingly, run cold during the summer and hot during the winter.

Even animals and birds were secure in their own environment before the partition of the country. It was considered a sin to kill any insect. The *mulla*, or priest, of our village mosque, Mohammed, was a very pious man who did not harbor any feelings of religious discrimination. He did not demand any compensation for leading prayers in the mosque, as is the practice nowadays. He used to work as an ordinary postman for a monthly salary of five rupees. He would collect the post from our schoolteacher, Moolchand, and from Bakhsho Laghari, and then deliver it all ten kilometers away to Tando Kaiser. He would promptly return for prayers in the mosque, always merciful and seeking mercy. Shias and Sunnis would offer prayers in the same mosque, and no one particularly cared if someone was folding their arms or folding their palms.

All this peace and harmony was suddenly shattered, and the balance of the entire village was threatened. Today I recall a storybook from my

Chapter 2: Memories: Village of Bakhsho Laghari

childhood. There was a great monster in one of the stories who kept crying, "scent of man ... scent of man ..." in his hunt to devour any human being that would be around. The present circumstances surrounding my beloved, once peaceful village, seem no different from this story. The religiously bigoted Mullas are after human flesh in everything but name!

With the partition, Hindu women would come with folded hands to bid goodbye to their lifelong Muslim friends and neighbors. Hindu men could be seen in the streets bidding a tearful farewell to their Muslim brethren. I had never seen my father shed a tear, but on that day, I saw him crying like a child! He kept on pleading with his Hindu friends saying, "Seth Thakumal, Seth Gehamam do not leave your homeland. We have so much in common ... our cremation grounds and graveyards have existed side by side." Those who left sadly replied, "Perhaps our share of water and food in Sindh has come to an end, but wherever we go we shall always cherish you and our fond memories." It must be an exceptional storm to uproot that many old trees. Who can withstand such a raging storm, which marked an end to generations of unity?

As Shah Latif has said: "The moments written by Fate are the only moments one is destined to live."

Chapter 3

Fatima's Childhood

Fatima was born on August 7, 1940 in Bakhsho Laghari. Fatima was raised as an orphan alongside her three brothers, as their father died unexpectedly when she was nearly four years of age. Her elder brother was about six years of age at the time of their father's passing, and her younger brothers were roughly three years of age and eighteen months, respectively.

At such a tender age, Fatima was forced to shoulder the household responsibilities to help her mother eke out a living for her family. She was responsible for looking after her younger brothers, often carrying the youngest in her arms, and calming them when they would become cranky. She would busy herself by cleaning the house, washing and arranging kitchen utensils, and lifting mattresses and sheets to prepare them for nighttime. When she washed clothes, she would take extra care to arrange each piece of clothing for each respective member of the family. When she grew older, she would also go to the fields to cut grain stalks, harvest onions, and collect them in a heap for her mother to sell. Fatima also offered her assistance to her extended relatives, running errands for family in the village with no fuss.

During the agricultural season, Fatima would eat her lunch before starting work and toil in the hot sun for many hours. She would busy herself by practicing embroidery and taking on sundry stitching jobs during the off-season, crafts which were essential for any girl to learn in those days. She would practice cooking, learning from the elders of the neighborhood. If she was ever given compensation for her work, Fatima would give it to her mother, asking for nothing in return. She never demanded new clothes or bangles even during Eid festivals, and she never complained about her torn footwear. Her relatives and her neighbors reserved nothing but the highest praise for her.

This life of hardship gave Fatima many practical experiences, even though she had not been formally educated. From a young age she proved herself to be responsible and capable, conscious of her duties. She was endowed by nature with many virtues.

The area of Bakhsho Laghari where the Ghanwani families resided was a congested locality consisting of about 20 square-shaped houses. Fatima's residence was three houses from our own. Her father, Chacha Murad Ali Khan, was a decent man respected for his courage and uprightness. He bore a distinct personality. Their elders were related to well-known and affluent families of the region who were quite well-educated; one of them was a chief engineer in the irrigation department, others were doctors, and one relative was a session judge.

Fatima's elder brother, Ahmed Ali, was enrolled in school; she had to be there for him and provide for his needs until she was married to me in 1958. Electricity did not reach the village until 1957. Before electricity was available, studies had to be conducted at night by lanterns or earthen lamps. Her brother studied agriculture and ultimately secured employment with the government.

Chapter 3: Fatima's Childhood

When Ahmed Ali was admitted into a school to pursue an education, the teacher at that school called my father and advised him to send me to school as well, or else those in charge of enforcing compulsory education would harass him. Fatima's brother and I thus started going to school from the Ghanwani neighborhood. Though Ahmed Ali was my elder by roughly two years, I somehow always maintained first rank while he maintained second in the class.

Allow me to dwell for a moment on the attitude toward education in those days, to provide additional context. In the vicinity of our village Bakhsho Laghari, there is a bus stop known as Makhan Moori, where some Pathan families resided. Those who were in charge of enforcing compulsory education called a Pathan man, Azim Khan, and told him to send his son to school to study. He stubbornly refused, and as a result he was sentenced to jail for 15 days or to pay a fine of 50 rupees. The higher authorities, thereafter, insisted that he follow the rule of the land. Azim Khan very innocently requested the presence of the authority to pay him 50 rupees, and he was prepared to be jailed for 15 days. At this, the person in charge was nonplussed and let the matter rest there.

Ahmed Ali and I were both sincere about our education, and we worked hard to maintain our ranks in school. Until the sixth standard, we were taught by a teacher who belonged to the Thakur caste; as we entered seventh standard—which was considered vernacular final—we were taught by another teacher named Mohammed Sidique Soomro. He was an able teacher and was from a place called Bhindo sharif. Yet another teacher, Habib Allah Soomro, was famous as well, and it was said that both were capable teachers for the final examination and that success was secured for anyone who sought private sessions with them four months before exams. Ahmed Ali and I both worked hard to pass our final exams, and we obtained good marks.

We continued with our studies but, at the time of the country's partition in 1947, the entire education system was suspended until 1949. Many teachers were Hindus and were forced to migrate south at that time. There were about 600 students on the school's roll before the partition, but attendance after the partition averaged only about 400 students. The school was left with six teachers, including one religion teacher who was employed to impart a religious education.

Chapter 4

Efforts for Fatima's Engagement

Sultan Ahmed Khan was selected as the chief of the Ghanwani clan after the death of his father and Fatima's uncle, Murad Ali Khan. He was responsible for the family's social obligations, including those of Fatima as her blood cousin. Fatima's mother visited Sultan Ahmed Khan and his mother one day, telling them that she had come to broach an important subject with both elders present. Her daughter, Fatima, had matured, and she believed that it was time to look for a suitable boy for her. Fatima's father would have arranged these affairs had he not passed away many years before, but having left Fatima's mother a poor widow, the responsibility was cast upon them. Daughters of the poor are quite vulnerable otherwise.

Sultan Ahmed Khan and his mother consoled her and said that such matters required careful consideration and that nothing should be arranged in hurry. It is easy to fall in a pit, but to emerge requires great efforts. With this counsel, they sent her back home. After she left, Sultan Ahmed Khan sought the counsel of his mother, Fatima's aunt. His mother suggested that he should move the matter to his father's sister, as her son had become recently widowed, and he was without any issue. Sultan Ahmed countered that the boy was a widower, and that he was considerably older than Fatima in age. He argued that they could do no such injustice to the girl; if her father were alive, it would have been at his discretion but, in his absence, it was their responsibility. That arrangement, Sultan Ahmed concluded, was inadvisable. His mother argued that the boy's family was quite well-to-do, and that the girl would inherit all the property.

Sultan Ahmed's mother visited the boy's house and moved the matter to the next day. The boy's mother told them that she wanted some time to think over the proposal. "You have to find the bride for your son," Fatima's aunt pointed out, "and in this bargain, you get the daughter of your own cousin. She is from a poor house, which will secure you not only a daughter-in-law, but the praise of even ordinary folk impressed by your large-heartedness." The boy's mother insisted that she needed more time to mull the proposed arrangement.

Fatima's aunt called an old woman from the village the next day and confided the news of the potential engagement with her. That old woman suggested that they should go to a soothsayer who had occult powers (the wife of a local *pir*, which in Sindhi loosely translates to a witch) on the following Friday to determine the suitability of the match. They consulted the soothsayer that Friday and after speaking with her in confidence, they were asked to return the following Monday. They complied, and on Monday they were asked to sit in a separate room while the soothsayer kept herself busy for some time. Finally, the soothsayer returned, telling them that her spells indicated that Fatima was destined to marry twice. The husband of her first marriage would die immediately, and she would later remarry as a widow. Thus, this first attempt to find a suitable boy for Fatima failed. This superstitious

Chapter 4: Efforts for Fatima's Engagement

news was bound to spread in the small village, and when it did, it only added to the woes of Fatima and her mother.

Sultan Mohammed and his mother were worried after all this and took time to ponder the matter. Sultan Mohammed suggested to his mother that her uncle's son was still unmarried, and to get him married to this girl who was both orphaned and poor would grant them divine blessings. She broached the subject, but the boy, Abdulkarim, flatly refused, saying that we wanted to marry a rich and beautiful girl. Sultan Khan told his mother after a few days that there was a very decent family in their neighborhood, that of his uncle Ghulan Khan. They lived only a few paces away from our own house, and while both families are poor, the boy himself was known to be disciplined and of good nature. Sultan Mohammed Khan mused, "We may solve the problem of both poor families in this way." He called my father then and told him to bring an engagement ring for the girl to formalize the engagement. This is how Fatima's and my engagement was announced, with the bestowment of a ring as a token and the distribution of sweets.

Chapter 5

Our Marriage

I anxiously awaited results after appearing for my final examination, and in the meantime I continued to help my father. I was very concerned about the poverty that we faced in our daily life. My education gave me insight with which I started to think about moving beyond this poverty. There were times when I would loathe myself and the fact that I could not be much help to my family after all the trouble my parents had gone through to educate me. I wanted to understand the reason for this state of affairs. Where did the problem lie? Father was not addicted to any vice like intoxication or gambling; he was sincere and a hard worker. He used to work in the fields of the landlords as a meager crop sharer. We had our own domestic animals, and we had grain and clarified butter (Ghee) for our own use at home. He was still, however, in a state of perpetual debt. When the results of my vernacular final examination were announced, I had secured 66 percent marks—this was considered a good result. My teachers, Mohammed Sidiq Sooro and Moolchand, called my father and told him that I was a good student who should be allowed to pursue further education. They advised him that education was the only path to transcend poverty. In the absence of education, they told him that his family would continue to be steeped in poverty and engage in backbreaking labor for the landlords, always trapped in debt.

My father was a victim of deprivation; he did not see any ray of hope, and he felt crushed under the weight of his debt. He had nothing with which he could bear the expenses of my higher education, which in those days was available only at Hyderabad or Tando Adam. He did not want me away from his supervision and in a strange place. My teachers, however, were insistent. They offered a cup of tea to us many times so that he might reconsider. They finally suggested that it would be better to find out from the student himself as to what future he desired for himself.

That is when my teacher, Mohammed Sidiq, asked me, "Do you want to study further, or you also want to wield a spade just like your father?" I very humbly thanked them for allowing me to speak in the presence of my father, and I requested that they forgive me for any inappropriate expression that I may use. I kept silent for some time, thinking. They all urged me to speak my mind. I told them that I was sure that they as teachers and my father all wished me a better future. "If my father would willingly allow me to go for higher studies, I assure you that I will do my best to acquit myself and meet the expectations placed upon me. I assure you that I will face all the difficulties and remain on campus." I continued: "If my father desires that I help him with physical labor and wants me under his supervision so that the family's financial condition improves, I am willing to abide by his wishes. I leave everything to God and my parents to decide my future. I crave His happiness alone."

My father got up in that moment and told me that he would like me to remain at home. It appears that my father had been sternly warned by

Chapter 5: Our Marriage

the landlord to repay a loan amount, and he needed the extra support from me in the fields. My teacher, Moolchand, had at this point offered to go with me to Hyderabad, settle me in a hostel, get me books, and pay the fees for my first term. My father simply thanked them and said that if he ever decided that I should be sent for higher education, he was sure that they would always be there to help.

When we returned home, we found my mother waiting anxiously for us. I was my parents' first male child after the birth of four girls in succession, and she was not ready that I should move away from her sight. My mother consoled me by saying that the boys who had studied only up to fourth standard were securing decent jobs, assuring me that I would get a much better job in the village having passed the final, seventh standard. God is merciful, anyway, she concluded, and assured me that He would gracefully look after our needs.

Mother had a valid point. A significant portion of the educated population had moved to India after the partition of the country in 1947, which meant that many jobs were available in the village to the less-educated local population. Ghulam Ali Laghari of our village at that time, for example, was an executive engineer in the irrigation department, and he had secured employment for some less-educated people.

My ambition for a higher education, thus, had come to naught, and I began to work with my father in the fields. I would read any scrap of newspaper or periodical that I would occasionally come across in the village; there was not a single educated or cultivated person in the village who would subscribe to any newspaper or periodical, so this was very rare. Any issue that I could find would be at least three days old by the time it reached our village, and it would be another three or four days before I could lay my hands on it.

My younger brother, Hussain Bux, later father to Amir Karim and Rassol Bux, lost ambition to study after I had to abandon my hopes to pursue a higher education. He completed an education only through fourth standard and left the school system when he was in fifth standard. I did not secure any employment and was in no place to help my brothers pursue a higher education. My father had only produced one-fourth of the produce that he did after my brothers and I joined him in the fields; we purchased our own bullocks, and began to keep half of the produce. We all turned our efforts to improving the yield.

During this time, someone recommended my name to Ghulam Allah Khan Laghari, who issued a letter for my training for irrigation. The letter was brought by Deh Buxo Laghari of our village, who was working in the department at the time. I was to train under him, in the village itself. I would train with him for six months of the year and would continue with normal work on the fields as well. Training letters were issued to others, too, but at the end of the training period only two were given regular duty, and all others would return to their usual work. My brother told me that I should not depend on false promises of unreliable people, as I had before, as my absence from the field had already adversely impacted our work. He recommended that I devote myself completely to the usual work to recoup the losses that had been suffered.

We got a message from Fatima's guardians after all of this, stating that it was time to solemnize the marriage and rid them of their social responsibility. Our marriage took place on April 8, 1958.

Our houses were in close proximity, as I stated earlier. We stayed for two days at Fatima's parent's house, and on the third day, we came to

Chapter 5: Our Marriage

live in my house. A new chapter of our life thus commenced. Fatima was born on August 2, 1940, and I was born on August 7th that same year. Fatima was my elder, thus, by five days. We both were eighteen years of age at the time of our marriage.

Fatima's responsibilities increased after our marriage. She adjusted rapidly to the new environment and family traditions as well as to the temperaments of her new family members. Fatima had an obsession with cleanliness and order and would run the house with thrift and efficiency. She would take care of the household chores and even look after the personal needs of her in-laws, especially my siblings who were younger than her in age. She considered my younger brothers as her own sons, in addition to the children of her own siblings. They would, in-turn, treat Fatima with respect, as though she were their own mother.

Chapter 6

An Addition to the Family

My father, mother, brothers, and I were all busy with our daily schedules. The men would work in the fields and, due to our work ethic, we were able to afford livestock—five buffalos and a number of goats. We were moving toward self-sufficiency. My mother and Fatima would take care of the household chores, and they both tackled their massive responsibilities head-on. God's mercy and sense of abundance was there.

We remember our times of deprivation and thank God for the merciful bounty. My mother would sometimes express her wish for a small addition—"a little angel"—in the family. I would console my mother by saying, "Have faith in the mercy of Almighty. His will shall be done."

One day, Fatima told me that the next time I went to market I should bring a special clay for her. Pregnant women crave this type of clay! My mother was very excited when I relayed the news to her, and she told me that a little angel was on its way. Fatima kept herself busy by making blankets and other clothes for the new arrival. At last, the much-awaited child was born at two o'clock in the afternoon on July

19, 1961. The child was healthy, and Fatima had no complications from the delivery. The child was shown to Fatima after the cleaning, at which point the village midwife instructed us to first whisper a prayer and say the child's name in his ear. We followed the instructions and whispered the name "Anwar Ali." We were steadfast in our decision that the child should carry the suffix "Ali."

While we had been married in the midst of poverty and could not adequately celebrate, the birth of a male child provided us with an opportunity to celebrate in a manner that fit the momentous occasion. Professional singers and dancers were invited, and we celebrated the occasion to our hearts' content. We believe that all glory and misery come from the hands of the Almighty, and we were grateful to Him for the opportunity provided.

Chapter 7

Trapped in a Feudal Setup

My family and I had not only mastered agriculture, but we became known for obtaining the best results. As a consequence, we were able to till the lands of various landlords, and our services were in great demand. My two younger brothers were also old enough to assist with cattle grazing. My father, uncles, brothers, and I were all working. We did not engage in any extravagant expenses, and we were free from any vice.

The river dam was breached in 1956, and the residents of a neighboring village, Haji Wikyo Khaskheli, took refuge in our village for about two months. Most of them returned to their village after that period, but one of them was a professional tailor who decided to open his shop in our village and settle there. He became quite friendly with my father, so I would go to sit at his shop when I was free. I would assist him with sewing buttons and with other chores of his trade. My father requested that this man train me as full-fledged tailor, since he noticed I was interested in the craft. For six months I concentrated on learning all that I could as the man took me under his wing, and at the end of this period, I was able to sew the typical garments for villagers to wear.

My father purchased a Singer sewing machine for me as a gift, to commemorate this development.

Fatima's cousin, Sultan Ahmed Khan, had a tea stall in the center of the growing village, along with an empty room near it. He offered this empty room to me so that I could start my own business with the sewing machine. I have always been able to adapt to the ways of rural culture, and just by sharing a cup of tea with any stranger, I can become one of their ilk and in this trade, that was the secret to my success. Within two years I had become a famous tailor who had more work than one could cope with. After considerable persuasion, I agreed to take on two assistants to whom I taught the trade.

My shop was part of a tea stall and as is commonplace in rural villages, it became a meeting place for the village idlers, gamblers, and hemp smokers. I managed to keep the crowd of gossipmongers away from my work, but I still felt suffocated in that setting. I did not own the establishment, however, and Fatima's cousins who *did* own it were themselves addicts who welcomed these activities. I was, thus, condemned to endure it all. I resolutely confined myself to my work for two years. I remained patient, did not complain, and I did not fall prey to any bad habits . . . at that point.

There came a time when the village witnessed an increase in the popularity of cockfighting. It was well-known that Sultan Ahmed Khan was an ardent fan of this sport, and he would often encourage me to bring his fighting cocks. Though I would initially resist his invitations, I finally succumbed to the vice; for all my talk, I was still a part of that rural-feudal culture. This sport adversely affected my work, and though I felt guilty, I could not stop. It became a full-fledged addic-

Chapter 7: Trapped in a Feudal Setup

tion. My father, brothers, and wife warned me and tried to dissuade me from the vice, but each day the car of a landlord, in the vicinity would come to the door and fetch me with my fighting cocks, which had been truly reared for fighting.

I became known as Rais Mohammed Ali Khan instead of being called Mohammed Ali as before. I would proudly visit many villages, and my shop would remain closed for days at a time. I was constantly being flattered. My customers left me and found another tailor, but I was a victim to addiction and remained oblivious to the financial losses, which were affecting my entire household. I would evade my father, who had no one to turn to so that he could complain about his own son. My brother was engaged in this period. Fatima struggled with her mental health and was under treatment for quite some time.

Fatima's condition is what came as a rude jolt to me, one that made me take stock of the situation and think about the direction in which my life was headed. My father had already sold two buffalos to pay for Fatima's treatment! She found herself pregnant again at this time, but she told me that she could not feel the child moving within her. I advised that she speak with my mother, knowing that she would speak with her own mother—my grandmother—who was a skilled midwife. I consoled Fatima, then, that she should not worry and that I would henceforth not go anywhere. My grandmother gave Fatima herbal medicines, and she soon went into labor and delivered another son.

I asked what name we would give the child, noting that while it was traditionally the practice that a father name his son, I believed that the mother who bears all the pain of carrying and delivering the child should have the prerogative of naming them. She answered by saying her eldest son was Anwar and that this son would be Munawar, with the suffix Ali, and thus our second son was named Munawar Ali. We whispered that name into the child's ears along with a prayer.

While we had been well-off and hosted celebrations with singers and dancers upon the birth of Anwar Ali, Munawar's birth had to be a more modest affair. We celebrated by cooking two pots of food and sharing the meal among close family. We were just grateful, above all else, that Fatima and our child had emerged from the ordeal safely.

After some time, my father told me that my engaged brother was the be married; his in-laws were insisting on solemnizing the marriage at the earliest convenience so that they might be free from their social obligation. I consoled my father, telling him that our merciful God would show us the way. We had already sold two buffalos for Fatima's treatment and were thus left with only two bullocks to plow the fields and nothing to sell. We decided to sell one bullock and keep the other so that, when the season came, a second one could be borrowed from someone. We had to exercise patience, as auctioning the bullock would not have exposed our dire need for money but it would have fetched an inferior price. We were able to sell the bullock and arrange my brother's marriage on a very modest scale, comparable to my own marriage.

Munawar's health began to take a serious turn at this point, to which Fatima suggested that the marriage be postponed by a week or ten days. Invitations had not been sent to relatives who were far away, since the marriage was such a modest affair, and so we notified those in the village who had been invited. We continued our vigil over the sick

Chapter 7: Trapped in a Feudal Setup

Munawar, and there came a point when our efforts and prayers were rewarded. We continued to administer the medicines as prescribed by the doctors for a long time and, with grace of God almighty, our child's life was spared.

Chapter 8

Crisis after Crisis

Fatima told me to proceed with my brothers' marriage ceremony as Munawar's health improved. It was a simple matter to cook and distribute some food among close relatives as well as give some clothes. My brother Hussain Bux's marriage to Mirzadi was as austere as our marriage was; if no one had cause to boast about this marriage, no one had cause to complain either. In poor households such as ours at the time, it is not the pomp and ostentation that matters; rather, true love, affection, and respect are what matter. I can confidently say that the family was very happy. My sister-in-law was very closely related to my wife, Fatima. Her father was Fatima's grandmother's sibling by blood. Fatima was, thus, happiest of all the family members for the marriage. Many relatives visited to congratulate my brother.

Although my mother suffered from asthma, she was able to do household work but with increasing difficulty. Fatima was burdened with raising Munawar who was a sickly child. Fortunately, Mirzadi proved to be very hardworking, so my mother and Fatima found her to be a great helping hand. Hussain Bux and Mirzadi, by the grace of God, were blessed with a son within a year or so. We were leading a happy and modest life, but bad days then befell us.

Hussain Bux was persuaded by some mischief-makers that he and his wife were doing all the work of the household while all credit was being usurped by his brother and sister-in-law—Fatima and me. He became jealous, and after the birth of their child, his wife returned to her parents' home, as per custom. However, she did not come back, and she persuaded my brother to stay with his in-laws, who bought him land for tilling. He was very confused, but silently consented to the situation as he could not oppose his wife or his in-laws. Father would lament that it was "woman gossip" that had brought forth the unfortunate situation. My brother expressed complete helplessness against his wife's adamancy that this must be done, even when others from the family or his friends would counsel him. Hussain Bux would toil all day long in his field, henceforth, but he eventually became ridden with debt.

Meanwhile my father, two brothers, and I continued to work our three fields. About one year after Hussain Bux left, at the recommendation of Rais Khuda Bux Khan of our village, I secured a job with Alam and Brothers as a bus conductor. In those days, a job as a conductor was considered a respectable job on par with any petty government official. In addition to the usual salary, it entitled one to commission and other allowances as well as the opportunity to obtain a loan if necessary. Buses would take people between Hyderabad and Dighri via Matli, moving through Tando Ghulam Ali, Tando-Aihar, and other places of importance. I gained the confidence of the owners within just six months by continuing to deliver higher returns than the other conductors whom they employed. Within a year my family and I emerged from abject poverty, and I returned to the village.

Chapter 8: Crisis after Crisis

I learned then that my brother, Hussain Bux, was not doing well. My father, mother, and I went to his in-laws' home and grabbed his sons (they had been blessed with one more child in that year) and announced that they would be moving out. I sternly told my brother not to take anything from the house, such that even their personal belongings were left behind. When my brother revealed that he had fallen into debt, our father said, "We will discharge all the debts. Let all those he owes come and collect their dues. Where the land is concerned, we shall not claim any compensation from the landlord." We called all those who had to be paid and brought my brother with his family back to our own house. How could we not? He was of our own blood! I realized that, while he had not separated from the family, he had been concerned about his reputation and a sense of self-respect, which had prevented him from returning home.

I said prayers of gratitude to the Almighty. I spent some days of my leave with family and relatives and was preparing to go back to my work. Fatima advised me that a vacant piece of land adjacent to our house was available and that I should try to get a new house built on that piece of land. The work needed to be started, as the family was growing. After discussing the matter with the elders of the family, I told her to go ahead with the project. I gave her some money to start the work and promised to send more money to her for that purpose. Father also enthusiastically took to building the new house. I assured him that I would be sending additional funds. As a last order of business on my leave, I met with my children's teachers to check in on how they were faring. Satisfied by the feedback I received and all that was happening in the family, I went back to my job at Hyderabad.

In the village, Father commenced the construction of the new house. It was decided that rooms should be quite commodious and that the house should have a big courtyard so that children could even play a game of cricket. Once when the work on the roofing of the house was underway and concrete was being poured, just as Munawar came outside, some concrete fell on his head, and he was injured. It took quite some time for his wound to heal.

Munawar was very dear and near to his uncle, Mohammed Bux. He used to follow us like a shadow, be it in the field or anywhere else. My father got him a baby goat, which he would play with and take everywhere. He became very attached to his pet goat. Seeing such a deep attachment his mother told him, "It is good to love animals, but if you get attached to your pet, how will you study and progress in life? You will merely herd the animals!" Fatima advised my father to sell that goat. The amount that he got from selling the goat was given to Munawar who, in turn, passed it on to his mother.

Chapter 9

Education of Children

I had led life in poverty and with a sense of deprivation. For a time, there was no hope of receiving help from any relative or any other source. I had, in a way, lost the hope of leading a decent life free from want. In our poverty I realized that my father could not afford a good education for me, even though I was a good student and deserved it. I firmly believed that it was those people who were steeped in ignorance that had been the barrier between an enlightened life and a decent life.

When I visited doctors' offices, I would see framed degrees and name plates on their walls and would take those as a challenge. I decided that my children and my brother's children would be educated without gender discrimination. This was my way of exacting revenge on an illiterate society bound in a web of superstition and tradition. I got my son admitted to a village school, and I bared my heart to his teacher at the time, Mohammed Bhurgiri; the teacher assured me that, with the grace of God, all would be well.

After some time, I confided in my son's mother, Fatima, and expressed that it would not be possible for us to emerge from the mire of poverty without a good education. I told her that the mother's role is of the utmost importance in this endeavor and that she had to be strict with her children in respect to their studies. She readily agreed and said, "I am myself uneducated. Without your enlightenment on this issue I would have committed the same mistake that normally mothers are apt to do out of love." I told her that I was not prepared to tolerate any leniency in this respect.

After some time, when I realized that Anwar had become used to regularly attending his school and that he was able to understand basic concepts, I shared my views with him. I told him that we were poor people and we had not inherited any ancestral property; any inheritance had been lost due to luxurious living and vices such as gambling and intoxication. We had no assets that could be invested in setting up any business for him. I told him that his grandparents would affirm my sentiments if he doubted the truth of my statement. In this way I impressed upon him the importance of education—the only vehicle to lift our family out of poverty. That education is sometimes ridiculed in the feudal society is only an obstacle on the road to our progress. I expressed how essential it was that he should not neglect his studies, for this was the only asset that we could bequeath to our children. I further told him to keep his needs within reasonable limits. These conversations continued for quite some time.

I sensed afterward that Fatima was being too soft on him, a result of maternal instincts against a strict pursuit of studies. I warned my wife against such an attitude, but she shielded him, saying, "He is a mere child. He will become serious when he grows up." I told her that I also

Chapter 9: Education of Children

loved him equally as he was my child as well, but that being soft at this age would prove detrimental to his own interest.

One morning, when I returned from working in fields, I found that Anwar had missed school and was playing marbles with vagabond children of neighborhood. I was resolved that we could not give an excuse in the future to our relatives, saying that "we tried our best, but our son was not interested in studies." I reprimanded Fatima for the severity of the lapse. I immediately called Anwar and was about to thrash him when his mother intervened. I asked him to pick his book bag, and I led him to school. I pleaded with his teacher not to punish him as I had punished him enough. I requested that someone be sent to call Anwar to school should he be absent in the future—I then assured the teacher that this future would never come to pass.

From that day onward Anwar started taking a serious interest in his studies. I never again received any complaint from his teacher about his being negligent in his studies.

Munawar came of school age four years later. Like his brother, Munawar initially started playing truant, but Munawar was less haughty and more intelligent. Once, when Munawar missed school and was being reprimanded, he accepted his mistake, meekly sought forgiveness, and promised not to repeat such a mistake in future. Both boys continued with their studies in a systematic manner, and I had no occasion to bother them again about their education. Just one incident remains, one which I hope they both remember as well.

Everything that I told them was for their own good. My relationship with my sons always has been rather friendly. I have enjoyed an especially good rapport with Munawar as both of us are witty. There are times, however, when Munawar's wit does not evoke laughter as desired. At times when I would joke with Fatima, her sons would also not lag behind; at that point, she would in mock-anger reprimand them. They would meekly ask for her forgiveness.

Chapter 10

From Bakhsho Laghari to Hyderabad

Anwar completed his primary education, fifth standard, in 1972, and I had to seek arrangements for Anwar's higher education. I asked Fatima about this, and her response was, "I am a woman. What can I do?" I told her that we can share responsibilities. She had to talk to the women in the family if Anwar were to live in Hyderabad, and I needed to convince Fatima's male cousins.

Anwar was settled at Landlord's (Rai's) house, and Fatima asked me what living arrangements I envisioned for Anwar as he pursued higher studies. She mentioned that her nephew would be moving to Hyderabad for higher education the following year and that we should consider finding a permanent arrangement for them. To do so, it would be necessary to have our own accommodation in Hyderabad.

The kitchen in our village home used to be a meeting space for members of the family to discuss important issues. This was where we would exchange views, share jokes, and plan our daily schedules. We decided here that it would be most prudent to ask Fatima's nephew's family if they would accommodate Anwar for one year in Hyderabad; in the meantime, we would get our own house in Hyderabad. That year would be a breather for us, on one hand, and provide ample opportunity to secure the necessary arrangements including furniture for the new house. Fatima complained about how we could furnish a new home in Hyderabad when our newly constructed home in the village did not even have complete furnishings or the necessary appliances. I promised her that we would address both matters by the time we moved in the coming year. The year would additionally give us an opportunity to find arrangements where both boys could stay. This would institute a good system of moral support for Anwar.

Fatima refused to approach Haji Hussain Bux's household about accommodating Munawar as she had approached them for Anwar—and those people were related to her by blood. She said that as Hussain Bux's mother was my cousin and I was his favorite relative, I should attend to this task. It is a question of only one year.

Coincidentally, Hussain Bux came to oversee his fields in the village. During a conversation, I shared my problem with him and asked him to accommodate Munawar at his Hyderabad house. He said he would consult his family members and get back to me. This reply did not satisfy Fatima, and she was pessimistic. However, as he promised, he consulted his wife and she wanted to know his opinion. He said that the boy would prove to be a household asset as he would help in sundry chores. His wife told him that had he refused in the first instance, he would have been held responsible for refusal but now in the village, she would be held responsible in case of refusal. In this way the problem of Munawar's stay was resolved. My wife was happy and at the same time, she credited herself for giving sane advice.

Chapter 10: From Bakhsho Laghari to Hyderabad

Anwar and Munawar both started going to Noor Mohammed High School. When she brought them, Fatima stayed in Hyderabad for a week to be comfortable with the arrangements. She left for the village after thanking the hosts and telling them to look after her sons as their own.

I continued with my duty as a bus conductor and would visit my sons in the evening. I would return to my own quarters after spending precious time with them and giving them a bit of pocket money. Fatima, meanwhile, kept herself busy by purchasing furniture for our new house in Hyderabad. We had a good yield that season and made a good profit. She purchased everything from bed sets and mattresses to a refrigerator and even a television set. This all had to be temporarily kept in our village home, as we did not yet have a house in Hyderabad. Televisions were not uncommon in cities by that time, but they were certainly a novelty in the village.

Munawar was responsible for providing water for the house while at Hussain Bux Kahn's residence in Hyderabad. They used to get water by using a water pump on the ground floor. Munawar would have to perform this duty at one o'clock in the morning, as the timings of the water supply were very odd. He could only sleep after this task had been accomplished each night. Once, when switching on the water pump, Munawar sustained a severe electric shock. That was the third time in his eleven years of life that God had intervened to save his life.

The one year of separation came to a close, and Anwar passed his matriculation examination with flying colors. Fatima's maternal uncle's two sons were also studying at Hyderabad. Elder Shahid Khan used to work for Dalda Ghee Corporation, and the younger one used to stay at her aunt's place belonging to Haji Shafi Mohammed Khan. Aslam used to be in the same class as Anwar, and they passed their matriculation examinations at the same time. Fatima's two uncles decided to get accommodation in Hyderabad, and I was told that we should stay together at the same place so that the rent and electricity bill could be divided equally. My wife Fatima further added that Aslam did not want to study alone, as he had been with Anwar throughout school, and his company would be a morale booster for him. Aslam considered Anwar and Munawar as his brothers. Fatima sought my advice on the matter. I told her that her decision mattered more, cautioning only that we needed to be careful so as to not create an issue and social complication in the future over any trivial matters. "I do not want to save money at the cost of creating ill will among relatives," I said, adding that she should not be wary of spending more than her share as delicate human relations matter more than money.

We decided to stay together. Both were successful in finding a suitable place to stay, and I paid the required advance amount. When I asked my wife when the best time for her to move into the new house would be, she replied that as all days belong to God, any one day was as good as any other day.

I summoned all the family members before formally leaving for Hyderabad. The meeting consisted of my father, mother, and both brothers' wives. I said it was imperative for Fatima to be at Hyderabad to look after the growing boys who were engaged in further studies. I apprised them about the problems that would arise from having two separate establishments at different places, including the obvious financial burden. The brunt of the household chores, meanwhile, which until that point were shared, would need to be shouldered by Mirzadi. By

Chapter 10: From Bakhsho Laghari to Hyderabad

then, my mother was old and would be able to help only a little. There was an enormous amount of household work at the village home; in addition to cooking for family members, Mirzadi would be responsible for cooking for the farmworkers and guests whenever they arrived. I was entirely confident that Mirzadi was capable of undertaking this responsibility. I entrusted one of my brothers with the task of moving furniture and settling the family in the new house at Hyderabad. Fatima and I ultimately decided to rent houses in Hyderabad, and thus in our time there, we moved from Liaqat Colony to Tando wali Mohammed and then again to another place near Mausoleums of Mirs. After six months, one of Fatima's nephews said that he was not able to bear the financial burden of staying in a separate house and he wanted to move out and be with his brother Aslam. I thought that one more mouth to feed would not pose much of a problem but would emerge as an educated person.

Aslam and Anwar were both admitted to the Government College of Kaari Moori and opted to study biology. The boys would visit the village during holidays. During one visit, Anwar's liver become infected, and he fell sick. By then, my sister was married and living in the village of Gulab Laghari, and her son, Rashid, who was nearly Anwar's age, came to visit him. Rashid sought my permission and blessing to return to his home that evening. I advised him to stay overnight and not to rush, but he said he needed to attend to his work and departed. We found him badly mutilated just 40 minutes later; the Datsun vehicle in which he was traveling collided with a heavy truck, which had caused a serious accident. I rushed Rashid to the Civil Hospital at Hyderabad in critical condition, but the doctors there declared him as "dead on arrival." I had to carry his body to my sister's home in the village of Gulab Laghari.

I cannot describe the distress that this accident caused me. I was devastated, as I could not bear to see the young boy—a prince charming—laying dead at the feet of his distraught parents. I had to accept it as God's will, but within two months, I was afflicted with tuberculosis. The bleeding was profuse, but I was cured of it after nine months of treatment in Karachi.

Chapter 11

Some Steps Toward Prosperity

I continued to perform my duty as a bus conductor and kept watch on the progress of Anwar's studies. Munawar continued to go to school, and I secured admission for my nephew as well. I assured him that I would treat him as my own sons and, as far as education was concerned, he would not face any discrimination. He and Munawar would go to school together and return together. They would help their grandfather and uncles in their field once they had completed homework and all sorts of work assigned to them. At times Munawar would collect grain from the floor and sell it to the shopkeeper in exchange for a slate or a notebook that he needed for schoolwork. He was rather obstinate and hotheaded and when angry, he would smash anything that he came across. Once, when a restaurant owner insulted him, he could not bear it. He climbed the roof in retaliation and started throwing stones, which caused the owners' customers to scatter. When I learned of this incident, I not only apologized to restaurant owner but got him new crockery as compensation.

One day, a friend of mine from Tando Quasir came to visit. After a customary lunch, the conversation veered to the topic of Tando Quasir as the center of the mango trade to Punjab as well as Quetta and other important trading centers. We decided to get involved in this trade and purchased the entire mango producing gardens in our respective villages for export purposes—creating a monopoly. I realized while engaged in this business that, in spite of my own honesty, the landlords would often sell inferior goods and try to cheat us.

Munawar once said, "As you are in the business of selling mangoes, give me some and I will sell them in the open. I will give you your dues, and I shall myself retain the profit." Munawar saved some money in this way. He approached the village barber for his own circumcision ceremony. The village barber demanded 200 rupees, but Munawar bargained with him and settled the matter at 100 rupees. Munawar reached home and—without indulging in any religious and social formalities—he completed his religious responsibility on his own. He did not want to indulge in customary celebrations and unnecessary expenses. His grandfather applauded him for his bold step.

Chapter 12

Brothers to be Married

By now I had left the job as a conductor and was busy in the orchid business. I started feeling uneasy with business, however, so I withdrew from the venture. I continued to guide the operations related to the land from Hyderabad. My brothers decided that we should purchase a tractor for the fields, and it arrived within four months. I told my brothers to find a suitable driver to take the tractor to our village, which was promptly done.

One day, in Hyderabad, Fatima and I were discussing sundry matters when she said that my younger brothers had come of age, suggesting they needed to be married and settled in life. They said that they had always respected her as their own mother. My brother Mohammed was hardly eight years of age when Fatima entered our home as a newlywed bride. She volunteered to find the match for Mohammed and said that it would be my responsibility to find a suitable match for Ganhwanr Khan. When I asked her if she had anyone in mind for Mohammed, she replied that her uncle's daughter, Aslam's sister, would be an ideal bride for him. She said that she was sanguine and that the family would accept if approached with the proposal. I told her to try it her own way.

One day, Fatima told me that her uncle had come to see his son Aslam. She had broached the subject of a marriage between his daughter and my brother. My sister-in-law, Mirzadi, was his sister's daughter, and thus his family was closely woven to ours. Her uncle responded that our house was most near and dear to him and that Mohammed Khan was virtuous indeed. He asked for a few days to finalize matters at his home.

I told Fatima to find the match for my other brother, too, so that the marriages might take place at the same time which, apart from other hassles associated with a marriage ceremony, would reduce our expenses. She told me that another girl in our neighborhood was a daughter of her cousin, Abdul Karim Khan. It was holy month of Ramzan, and during the Eid holidays, we all went to visit our village. We reunited with our relatives and met with Fatima's uncle, who after a conversation about the arrangement told Fatima that "now boy and girl both belong to you." Her uncle purchased sweetmeats for 500 rupees and formalized the engagement. The next day we visited for tea and gave a cash gift for the girl. We left after about an hour, at which point I asked about Abdul Karim Khan. I was told that he was at his home, so my father, mother, and I decided to visit. After the customary greetings had been exchanged, they inquired as to my reason for bringing my father and mother to their home. I told him to ask my father, to which my father responded that our family were their poor siblings and neighbors for a long time. He expressed that he had come hoping to find a hope shared among siblings, alluding to a proposal between the man's daughter and my younger brother. Abdul Karim and his wife asked for some time to think over the matter.

Chapter 12: Brothers to be Married

Two or three days later, they consented for a wedding proposal and sent a message that we could come and distribute sweets to formalize the engagement. Fatima happened to be in the village, as we were still celebrating the Eid holidays, so she organized the customary ceremonies of songs and dance demanded by such a joyous occasion. In the village and at our Hyderabad residence, many people came to congratulate us for this good news. Even my mother-in-law was busy entertaining guests who came to offer congratulations.

Fatima and I had by this time moved to our Hyderabad residence in Pathan colony. We had a surprise visitor one day, Ali Mohammed Khan, the son of Nabibux Khan Baloch, who was accompanied by his wife Zaibualnisa, the daughter of the respected Allah Khan Laghari. We extended a warm welcome to them for visiting our modest abode and offered them customary hospitality. They sat there for some time and during the conversation they inquired as to how much rent we paid for our dwelling. We informed them that it was 600 rupees per month. They offered that we could move into their house in Hyderabad for the same amount as rent and insisted that they would not take any deposit from us. We told them that there was a vast difference between our social position and theirs; they occupied much higher position socially than we occupied, so we were apprehensive about the proposal. What if, after some time, they asked us to vacate? That would be a difficult situation. At their insistence we agreed to move to that home on the first day of the next month.

I am very personable and socially amendable by nature, which means I had gathered quite a sizable circle of friends and acquaintances. I was often invited to participate in social occasions, such as weddings and funerals. This added to my social standing in the community, and I had earned the respect of those around me. All the while, I was conscientious to not become arrogant, which would invite the wrath of my creator. I would always pray and seek His mercy, and I tried to follow the virtues exhibited by Imam Hussain of Islam. Each year I would sacrifice a handsome bullock in His name, an act which would give me a sense of spiritual fulfillment.

One day, Fatima told me that, as a consequence of our heightened social standing, numerous guests were visiting both our house in Hyderabad as well as our village home. This was increasing the workload for the women of the family, and in the village, Mirzadi was facing the troubles alone. Fatima warned that the stress may affect her health, to which end she suggested that we expedite my brothers' weddings since both had been engaged for some time at that point. My mother also expressed her wish that her sons be married promptly. Fatima also suggested that Mirzadi should move to our Hyderabad house once my younger brothers were married to help her look after the increased workload there. I was in full agreement with Fatima on this score.

I reached out to the two girls' parents and after one month, we had chosen a date for the marriages. Invitation cards for the weddings of both my brothers were printed and distributed among relatives and friends during this period. I wanted these weddings to be celebrated on a good scale, to repay the social debt and gain the blessings of my aged parents. For hundreds of years, our family had been mired in grim poverty and previous marriages, including my own, had taken place on a very modest scale; now, however, God had bestowed his mercy upon us, and we were considerably well-off. Anwar wanted to call a renowned singer, Mohammed Yusuf, to perform on the occasion, but for some reason, he was unable to attend. Numerous singers were

Chapter 12: Brothers to be Married

invited instead and, by the grace of the Almighty, all went well. After the ceremonies I offered my prayers of gratitude to God, and I even contributed money to charity for His continued grace and mercy.

Hussain Bux Khan once described his memory as follows: "The marriage was performed at such a grandiose scale that it could not be repeated, even if one wished for it to be."

Chapter 13

Ups and Downs of Life

Fortune turns like a wheel. I am always apprehensive of the future, to which end I pray each day to the Almighty. I pray that He may grant me patience and a sense of contentment, and I pray as well that I may be spared from any adverse trial. These prayers give me the strength which I need to face my daily life. I remember the words of the immortal poet Shah Latif, who beseeched the creator to cover faults with the shield of His grace.

My mother and father were both from very poor families and orphaned, thus devoid of the love and affection of any parents-in-law. Poverty was such that, in a home without the name of God, there was nothing. Regardless of the state of her health, my mother had been condemned to perform virtually all household tasks, like fetching water, grinding grain, cooking, washing, and cleaning the home. My mother would remind us that there were no flour mills to grind the grain when she was younger, which meant she needed to manually grind grains in the millstone by herself. In those days, too, sugar commodities and related goods were rationed and in short supply. My mother would stitch our clothes also by needle with her own hands. She never expressed any desires to my father, who was engaged in a constant struggle to earn a simple living. If my mother fell ill, she needed to rely on faith healing or home remedies.

My mother delivered a total of nine children in her lifetime: four girls and five boys. Two girls and one boy died in infancy, due to a lack of proper medical aid, which meant I had two surviving sisters and four brothers. She once called me to convey that each of her sons were equally dear to her, and that each day she would pray for our well-being. She had one request to make of me one day, I told her that her word would be a command for me, whatever it was; she need only express her wish, I promised, and I would fulfill it at any cost. "Your brother, Ghanwar Khan, wants you to purchase a passenger bus for him," she said. I told her that I worked as a conductor; my job at that point was one thing, and that to run a bus service was a separate experience entirely, but I assured her that I would fulfill her wish.

Initially, I wished to consult my father about the proposal but, fearing he may scold my mother for having made such a demand, I took my brothers into confidence. I personally felt as though this step would invite financial disaster, but nevertheless I arranged to send one lakh of rupees to my mother so that my brother might go ahead with his plans. The secondhand bus was paid for with a down payment as well as monthly installments of four thousand rupees. We were financially drained already, having incurred the expenses of the grand wedding ceremonies for my brothers.

The passenger bus started to run the route on Sheikh Barkyo Road via Hyderabad to Tando Mohammed Khan. We secured a trusted driver and cleaner, as per our reputation. The bus was in good condition, with acceptable appearance and good tires, but we did not know that the engine and other repair work had been carried out on only a temporary basis. The bus started to give trouble within a month. The brakes would often fail, which at times resulted in it being stalled for days at a time. Sometimes, it would even stop midway during a trip and cause trouble to the passengers. The circumstances meant that we endured a loss that we truly could not afford. A thought to dispose of the draining vehicle crossed my mind, but my ego would not allow me to give up. The situation caused my brothers and friends to estrange themselves from me, which caused me great anguish. I had, after all, finally lifted the family out of grim poverty to the respectable middle-class level; unfortunately, this bus consumed all the profits from our harvest and livestock.

Finally, I sold the bus to a scrap dealer and settled my dues in 1988 before the riots unleashed by Mohajirs. Thus, I found myself in the same position from which I had once started to build. This one wrong endeavor proved very expensive to me, as if all my previous efforts had come to naught.

Chapter 14

Father Afflicted with Cancer

It was October 1983 when my father expressed that he was suffering from failing eyesight in addition to a nagging stomachache. He usually possessed an enormous capacity to bear any pain, and it was strange that he should complain. I mentioned this to my brothers who all advised me to consult Anwar, who at this point was already in the Liaquat Medical College, or LMC.

Anwar suggested that it would be better to bring my father to Hyderabad, where good medical care was available. He sent this suggestion through Munawar, who came to the village. So, we brought my father to our Hirabad residence at Hyderabad. We first consulted one specialist about his eyesight followed by another for his stomach ailment. My father began to take the prescribed medication, but he did not experience any relief for his symptoms. He endured the pain. My father tried to convince Munawar to bring him back to the village, but Munawar dissuaded him saying, "This is also your own home. It is easiest to consult doctors as needed should you remain here."

My father's condition deteriorated throughout the next week. Specialists were consulted, and they advised further tests, including an ultrasound. The ultrasound scans revealed that he was inflicted with stomach cancer. This came as a rude shock. I was almost tearful. I told Anwar to arrange for a private room in the hospital. I stayed with my father, and Anwar would visit after he was free from his classes. My father's condition continued to decline to the point that he had problems passing urine. His condition took a serious turn, at which point a tube was inserted to take out his urine. He again requested Munawar to take him to the village, and this time we complied. An ambulance was arranged to transport him.

I took him to the village, while Anwar promised to follow us next day as he had to attend a marriage of his friend, Mumtaz Shah. Munawar was enraged at his brother's behavior, but Anwar remained firm in his prioritization. Munawar and I brought my father to the village home on February 1, 1984. Some other relatives accompanied us there.

My father breathed his last breath and returned to his creator on February 4, 1984. He was a symbol of hard work, honesty, and integrity. He would always bless me, asking that God almighty not bring the day where I needed to stretch out my hand for help from anyone. On the third day of his death, a neighbor also died. Shahid. Khan, who, due to his nature was known as Raja (King), had died on the same day as my father. In this way two very great men departed from the neighborhood.

Chapter 15
Stepping into Politics

Anwar was in LMC, and Munawar had reached tenth standard by 1980. Munawar had taken a liking to debate and elocution competitions; he would take part in them at the school level. I would help him write his speeches and provide him with debating points. He would excel on the stage as a result of his hard work and preparation.

The Sindhi Nationalist Movement, meanwhile, had been sweeping across the educational institutions of Sindh since 1972. This movement aimed to separate Sindh from Pakistan and create an independent state, and I personally resonated with the cause as an ardent admirer of the great Sindhi poet Shah Abdul Latif. Anwar became an active member of the Jiye Sindh Student Federation when he joined LMC. Agents from the state's intelligence agencies had already penetrated the organization at that point; these agents would provoke disturbances intended to shut down educational institutions, thus depriving students of the opportunities they may have accrued from an undisturbed education. They condemned an entire generation to darkness and ignorance.

Punjabi students established the New Sindhi Students' Organization to counter the Sindhi nationalist sentiments. They were equipped with arms and well-funded by state agencies to instigate violence on various campuses. In 1982, Mohammed Ali Sheikhi along with a companion attacked Qadir Magsi, the face of the Jiye Sindh student federation. The intent had been to murder Magsi, but he escaped with injuries. An innocent clerk of the university in the vicinity was also injured in the attack. The college was shut down, and Dr. Azim Almani, the principal of the college, was adamant that he would not re-open the college until all students involved in the incident were arrested. No investigation was ever opened, however, and warrants for arrest were issued to police stations across Sindh only for students associated with the nationalist movement—and Anwar's name was on that list.

In Pakistan it is common practice for a family member to be taken into custody in lieu of anyone accused of a crime, a practice which I have since learned is a strange relative to other countries. To this end, Ghulam Rasool Lashari, who was a police officer and an acquaintance of mine, rushed to our village to find me. The village elders sent him away with the assurance that I would present myself before him at my earliest convenience. I visited him the next day and told him that the arrest of Anwar alone would not result in re-opening the school, but that all students would need to surrender together. I told him that all students accused were educated, and that their futures were at-risk given the implications. I even cited the warrants that had been sent across Sindh and told him that my area of residence did not fall within his area of jurisdiction. This was political, and I had nothing to do with it. The man was obstinate and would not listen to reason. No other parents of students had been summoned—they were living comfortably in their homes—but he detained me under the pretense that I would be re-

Chapter 15: Stepping into Politics

leased only when Anwar surrendered himself to custody. No argument would budge him. I was in police custody for 14 days.

After 14 days, a student, Anwar Dodo Khan Rind, brought Police Officer Farooq to demand my release, arguing that it was futile to detain only one person. I was released by the police station but warned that I would be summoned again if necessary. One month later, an inspector from Jamshoro police station arrived at my doorstep and took me away to the station, where I found Qadir Magsi's uncle in addition to relatives of many other students implicated. We were detained for two days before we were presented before an army officer.

All accused students volunteered their surrender in this time frame and LMC college was at last re-opened. Fatima taunted me when I returned, saying that it was very brave of me to hand my son over to the police and return home with my head held high. I retorted that she should hold courage, too, that such brave sons were born of her womb.

Chapter 16

Fatima "The Sindhi Nationalist"

Fatima had two sons of her sister Mariam live at our Hyderabad house so they could pursue higher education. She was mother to many more. Practically all the children who came in contact with Fatima received maternal love from her, and they reciprocated in ample measure. During her sickness at Islamabad Hospital, Dr. Ismail Memon, Dr. Abdulah Memon, and Dr. Ghulam Hyder Zardari treated her as their own mother. During the six months that she was in hospital, her nephew Abdul Rehman Laghari did not miss a day visiting her with a gift of fresh fruits, and he would often say that she was not his aunt but his mother.

Fatima was changed by the events—her sons' hiding underground, their harassment by police, and their eventual imprisonment introduced a shift in Fatima's perspective. She was convinced that her sons were not capable of any violence and that Anwar had been falsely implicated in the case. She told Munawar that she would no longer respond with anger to their activism; she would instead be their comrade in arms, fighting for the just cause, which they espoused.

Munawar read Maxim Gorky's *Mother* aloud to her for two or three nights after she expressed her newfound conviction. The novel inspired her to take action; the conviction was not fleeting, and Fatima lived to her word. She began volunteering to paste posters on walls and distribute nationalist organization's flyers. She would not only feed her comrades but wash their clothes, and she tried to make them as comfortable as possible. Fatima volunteered to vacate her own room to accommodate comrades as necessary, to which end, our house in Hirabad became a refuge for all Sindhi nationalists. There, the needs of all nationalists were met, no matter which specific group or faction they belonged to. Fatima recalled from old Islamic history that women had been responsible for nursing the injured in the wars and, should the occasion arise, she was determined to rise to it.

Dr. Qadir, Nawaz Gahoti, Ghulam Hyder, and Anwar were eventually released from detention, and they continued their studies at Liaquat Medical College. The Sindhi Nationalist Movement, meanwhile, continued to gain strength each day. The center of the movement was at Sunn village, where Saeen G. M. Syed resided, but universities and other educational institutions remained the backbones of the movement. Sindhi nationalist students drove the movement, really, inspired to organize by the revolutionary zeal. Jamshoro University emerged as a particularly important center, beyond Hyderabad; Sindhi nationalist literature was published there, lectures were held, and a number of additional activities connected with the movement were conducted there. There were no doubt many additional centers across Sindh.

The movement to restore democracy was at its peak during Zia ul Huq's regime. In our Hyderabad home, Fatima would carry out whatever miscellaneous projects our sons assigned to her. The singer Bijal,

Chapter 16: Fatima "The Sindhi Nationalist"

a frequent guest, would record cassettes of nationalist songs. It was around this time when, near the Thori rail station, the army fired unprovoked upon a group of unarmed students. Many of the students who had been traveling from Mehran University to Lakarna in buses were killed instantly. A number of students were arrested in the wake of this staged incident, released after four to five years of detention. Countless students were subjected to painful lashings in a concentrated effort to suppress the Sindhi Nationalist Movement.

Munawar had reached college and distinguished himself as an able debater by this time. In those days, Saeean G. M. Sayed would celebrate his birthday in his village, Sunn, with a festival which his followers from across Sindh would attend. Students would flock from all universities to join in the sizable gathering. Once, in the midst of preparations for the celebration, a quarrel ensued between two groups of students at Sindh University. Qadir Magsi was asked to mediate and bring peace in those two groups, but mischief-mongers fired upon him when he was with his fellow students. Kamal Rahimoo died in this incident, and the attack left Dr. Krishan, Dr. Dawood Aatho, and others injured. To save their lives, Anwar and Dr. Humayoon took Qadir Magsi and other victims to a private nursing home, where they were operated upon, and their wounds were dressed. To save them from subsequent arrest they were brought to an underground shelter. Two or three of the students were brought to our Hirabad residence and Fatima was given the responsibility to look after and nurse them.

Anwar delivered the body of Kamal Rahimoo to his family after the post-mortem had been conducted. He then rushed to the national gathering in Sunn after performing the necessary customs and burial. When he returned from Sunn, all energies were directed to protect the lives of the injured from any unfortunate eventuality for which they were marked. The police had intensified their efforts to trace the whereabouts of Qadir Magsi, and at the behest of friends, he was brought to our Hiribad residence. His parents were strictly instructed not to visit him under any circumstances, and other family members were told to obtain permission in advance. Anwar would surreptitiously procure the necessary medicines to dress his wounds, using supplies from the nearby hospital to which he had access as a medical student. The medicine was sent through his younger first cousin, Karim, to hoodwink the authorities.

Intelligence agents shadowed suspect students each day. They realized that Karim would change the course of his movements at the end of each day, and they could sense that something unusual was afoot. They wished to find out what he was carrying. Whose errand was he running? When they discovered that Karim was carrying the materials for dressing wounds, it was not difficult for them to deduce that it was to aid a seriously wounded person who had taken refuge. They suspected at the time that it could be either the notorious *dacoit* Kashmir Khan or Qadir Magsi.

Finally, Qadir Magsi announced that it was time he changed his place of residence, to which end comrade Humayoon was called. Fatima was upset, thinking perhaps she had not taken care of him well enough. He reassured her that she had nursed him, washed him, and cleaned him as his own mother; he would always remember her as if she *were* his own mother, and he would always remain indebted to her. He was hounded by the police, however, he reminded her, and thus it was inadvisable to remain in any one place for too long.

Chapter 16: Fatima "The Sindhi Nationalist"

This discussion happened at midnight, and Humayoon came shortly thereafter. Amir, Karim, and Munawar were assigned to scan three directions to confirm that passage was safe. Humayoon and Anwar put Qadir Magsi in a chair and carried him in a fourth direction, to some unknown location.

When Fatima woke up the next morning, she found that the house was surrounded by police vehicles. She quickly awakened Anwar, who found that they had come in full gear and with all preparations. He woke up Amir and Karim as well, whose mother Mirzadi was also present at home. Mirzadi decided to protest and oppose them, determined that she would not hand the boys over to the police. She feared that they were young and, under pressure from the police, they may crack.

Munawar, Zubair Sheikh, and Aslam Ansari had been prepared to travel to Karachi that morning, and as expected they reached our home that morning. They turned back once they saw that the house was besieged by police, confident knowing that Qadir Magsi had already been shifted to another safe location. They thought it would be prudent to warn Qadir Magsi about the situation. When they arrived at the new location, any pretense that they knew of Qadir Magsi's whereabouts were initially denied, but Munawar and the others convinced them of their loyalty to the movement and informed them about the unfolding situation. Qadir Magsi decided in that moment that he should immediately be moved to another safe place.

The police, meanwhile, managed to secure a search order of our house and made the necessary preparations to mount a search. Fatima and Mirzadi were wielding kitchen knives to oppose the police force when they entered. They demanded that a neutral party be introduced to the force, and that if they defied that wish and entered forcefully they were prepared to kill and to be killed. The authorities were taken aback by this. They relented and asked to speak to any male present in the house, to which Fatima retorted, "If any male member was present, we would not have been compelled to face you in this way." The police argued that they had official orders to search the home. Mirzadi agreed to allow a search, but on the condition that it be conducted in the presence of an eminent and well-known person. They were justifiably concerned that the police force may plant something and falsely implicate them. The officers pacified them, asserting that they were men of honor, from respectable families whom they had to look after. They found only some materials for dressing wounds and bottles of Thatta syrup during their search.

The officers wished to take the male children of the house with them to the police station, on the basis of these findings. The demand was vehemently and physically resisted by the ladies of the house. Fatima had an altercation with one officer and Mirzadi slapped another officer in the face, demanding to know under which law the boys would be taken into custody. Fatima and Mirzadi occupied the vehicles when the boys were forcibly removed from the house. Fatima was physically thrown from the vehicle, but Mirzadi managed to push an officer whose arm was entangled in the belt of his gun to the floor. The exchange happened in full view of the public, yet no one possessed the courage to come to their rescue.

The operation had started at five o'clock in the morning and ending three hours later. The police officers took all three young boys—Munawar, Karim, and Amir—as well as Fatima and Mirzadi into custody.

Chapter 16: Fatima "The Sindhi Nationalist"

They were taken to the Jamshoro police station, and on the entire ride over Munawar kept threatening Amir and Karim to divulge nothing to the officers; if they failed to heed his warning, he would befittingly punish them.

Munawar introduced himself as Aslam Ansari, son of Dr. Ali Mohammed Ansari of Karachi, at the police station, insisting that he had only arrived the previous day. He had to leave for his home today. He provided them the phone number and address to Aslam's home and welcomed them to verify his statement. The officers contacted the number given, and on the other end, Aslam's mother confirmed the statement. She elaborated, expressing that she had sent her son to Hyderabad for an errand and demanded to know the reason for his detention. She demanded to speak to her son to find out the condition of his detainment and threatened a lawsuit should he not be released immediately. When they decided to release Munawar, he insisted that he had no money on his person to travel directly to Karachi and requested a minimum of 50 rupees. They released him and gave him 50 rupees.

Amir and Karim remained in custody. They maintained that they were both the sons of the woman who had audaciously slapped an officer and pushed a constable. They were subsequently subjected to third-degree torture by the officers, who were determined to find out if the *dacoit* Kashmir Khan or Qadir Magsi had been given refuge at their house. They were released that evening and somehow managed to return home in Hirabad.

The conditions for Sindhis in Hyderabad had become difficult by the beginning of 1985. The Pakistan People's Party (PPP) boycotted the most recent municipal elections, which meant the Mohajir Quomi

Movement (MQM) and General Zia ul Huq seized power. They were a militant organization of Urdu-speaking refugees who migrated from India after the partition of the subcontinent in 1947 to 1948. This resulted in increased armed attacks and atrocities committed against Sindhi-speaking people, many of whom would be found dead in street lanes each dawn. A person from the interior of Sindh would not dare to venture out sporting a traditional Sindhi cap. This was the extent to which panic was created.

Dictator Zia ul Huq was killed by a bomb within his aircraft on August 30, 1988. This instigated fierce Mohajir Sindhi riots the next month, on September 30, which resulted in 300 deaths on both sides. The attackers were nonchalant, freely roaming about the streets of Hyderabad to consciously strike fear into the hearts of the local population. An Urdu paper ran provocative headlines, which declared that the riots had been orchestrated by the organization led by Qadir Magsi. This led to First Information Reports about hundreds of associated activists being registered at seven or eight regional police stations.

In August 1988, my family moved from our Hyderabad residence to a new house at Jamshoro. I advised my sister-in-law, Mirzadi, to leave Hyderabad and, while she was initially resistant, she and her children returned to the village on September 30th. Anwar arrived at the Hyderabad residence with Hameed Memon and his wife the week before. Memon instructed his wife to remain at our house when he would go out and to consider Fatima and me as her own parents. Anwar and Hameed returned to village after September 30th.

I continued to stay with Fatima at LMC Colony, Bungalow No. 7. I received a phone call from a reliable source on October 6th, however,

Chapter 16: Fatima "The Sindhi Nationalist"

encouraging us to vacate our home within the half hour because our home was to be raided. Fatima and I immediately returned to our village by taxi, with no time to carry any of our belongings. I received a call from Nazar Mohammed Junejo about one week later to inform me that our belongings had been left on the road outside our house. I sent my nephew to pick up whatever had been left behind, though only books and miscellaneous items were found. I became increasingly concerned for the safety of my family.

I received the news that Karim and Ashan had been arrested at Dr. Mohammed Ali's flat on October 15th. I was deeply afflicted by the news, for Karim was my favorite nephew and his parents' darling. Karim was severely tortured while in custody and, though I tried to console his parents, I was anguished myself. We had no choice but to interpret the turn of events as bad fortune.

Anwar and Munawar, meanwhile, were both hounded by authorities, and the raids to capture them continued relentlessly. Fatima and I arranged for Anwar's engagement in this time period, as per the suggestion of Qadir Magsi. Anwar and Hamid were each offered interviews for employment at that time, with Anwar's scheduled in Hyderabad and Hamid's in Sukkar. Anwar managed to conduct his interview and return unharmed, but Hadim was arrested in Sukkar. I approached everyone who maintained some degree of influence with the authorities in response, urging that students be afforded better conditions and amenities while they were imprisoned. Meanwhile, Fatima and Mirzadi organized hunger strikes and protests outside police stations and prisons against unlawful arrest, and these combined efforts were responsible for securing better treatment in the jails.

The state in those days was governed by the Pakistan People's Party. Quarrels between native Sindhis and Muhajir immigrants continued unabated, and the incarceration of youth became common. The mothers of students who had been arrested began to approach party leaders as well as Saeen G. M. Syed who was the leader of the nationalist movement. The mothers became powerful agitators—thorns in the side of the party leaders; the tactics were deemed necessary to secure the lives of the children, and as this organizing bore some result, the women were inspired to continue.

The mounting fear meant that just a handful of native Sindhis would venture into the cities in those days, only risking the venture in cases of dire need. Landlords who usually stayed in Hyderabad fled to their village homes in panic. The woman and daughters of Sindh, however, continued to stand together, shoulder to shoulder with Fatima and Mirzadi, who continued to lead protests in front of police stations and press clubs. The progressive wing of the Sindhi Nationalist Movement organized a mass prayer one day for all those who had been martyred for the cause; a massive group of people across Sindh participated in the prayer meeting. Fatima and Mirzadi used the occasion to lead a march—hundreds of women strong—to facilitate a prayer meeting inside the grounds of the local hospital. Fatima advised me that the prayer meeting should be held on the open road outside the hospital and instructed me to lead the prayers. The gathering was converted into a procession after the prayers, which moved along Tilak incline, Hyder Chowk, S P Chowk and culminated at the press club. This was the first nonviolent procession in Hyderabad in many years.

Fatima had gathered a dedicated band of women workers around her by this point. This included Sister Gulnaaz, who was not only educated but fiercely dedicated to the cause. Pirha Sindhi, Marui Rustamani and Jamila Soomro were similarly striking in their work ethic and commitment. Comparable women's groups spontaneously emerged in many localities across Sindh. These women, including Jamila Soomro at Jacobabad and Naila Rahoopoto at Nawabshah-Khairpur, inspired many other women to join the movement as volunteers.

This was met with continued resistance by police in the cities of Sindh. Dr. Qadir Magsi and Humayoon Kazi were arrested at midnight on May 19th, 1989 from a bungalow in Gulistan Sajjad. The region erupted as the news spread across Sindh; workers, peasants, students, women, children, and senior citizens were protesting. Sindh was shut down for nearly a week. There were some among the protestors who resorted to arson as a form of protest and smoke could be seen for miles around. This massive surge of support offered solace to Fatima and Mirzadi, who realized that they were not alone in the movement: success was imminent.

The Sindhi people protested for seven days without any fear of being shot or dying. This conviction saved the lives of Qadir Magsi and Kazi Humayoon. The government yielded to the public pressure, finally admitting that they had arrested the two men. The public announcement caused the ladies from the households of both Qadir Magsi and Kazi Humayoon to get in touch with Fatima and become active members of the movement.

The events prompted the creation of a formal women's network that connected women within the movement across virtually all parts of Sindh. Its creation was guided by the hands of Gulnaz, Fatima, Mirzadi, and a handful of other women. The women's organization thus became a strong element of the movement.

Chapter 17
Gathering in Bhit Shah

Barely two weeks elapsed before the Prime Minister, Benazir Bhuto of the ruling Pakistan People's Party, held a public meeting at Hyderabad. He told the gathering that "If the entire province erupts into protests upon the arrest of terrorists, how will it be possible to restore peace?"

To reflect on the prime minister's absurd charge, a special meeting of Taraqi Pasand, the progressive party, was summoned. Gulnaz and Fatima were invited as representatives of the women's group. The decision was made after much consideration to invoke the great poet of Sindh—the *soul* of Sindh, Shah Abdul Latif—in a mass gathering on June 28th. Together, we would pray to his spirit to grant us courage and to lodge a complaint against the atrocities being perpetrated against his children by mighty rulers and to invoke divine justice. We were intent to declare:

"WE ARE NOT TERRORISTS BUT WE ARE REAL PATRIOTS AND PROUD BEARERS OF [SHAH ABDUL LATIF'S] LEGACY."

I was appointed Press Secretary of the Progressive Party at the gathering and elected as a convener of the committee to organize this event at Bhit Shah. I was also nominated as a patron and a leader of the women's wing (Nari Tehrik) along with sister Gulnaz. Copies of this resolution and details for the planned event were duly sent to the press across Sindh. We had a goal that the number of women present should be equal to the number of men, and many women volunteers, led by Gulnaz, mobilized other women to participate in the event. We could not inform our friends who were lodged in various jails across the province of Sindh; there was a strict rule that no weapons of any kind could be carried, nor could any slogan be shouted. These instructions were conveyed to the cadre of the party from time to time. It was decided that volunteers and participants could only carry the flag of the Progressive Party on the occasion.

About 11 or 12 buses from Bharia reached the venue on June 28th. Their entry was unique and deserves to be immortalized. All participants were clad in black clothes, barefoot, and they marched two persons together raising the slogan:

"YAA ALAH YA RASOOL QADIR MAGSI BE QUSOOR"

(O! God O! Prophet! Qadir Magsi is innocent!)

This slogan was later appropriated by the Pakistan People's Party for their partisan interests. Participants will to this day vouch that the gathering was not one with less than 100,000 people in attendance. The equal participation of women was achieved, thanks to the hard work and dedication of Gulnaz and her team, which meant this was the first gathering where more than 50,000 women had congregated.

Chapter 17: Gathering in Bhit Shah

Comrade Hussain Bux snatched a piece of paper from my hand and pocketed it. He told me that as a senior member of the movement, I should address the meeting at the end, sensing that I may pre-empt the others in my enthusiasm. Gulnaz Laghari delivered a splendid and memorable speech, one that could be compared only to one that I had heard delivered at the function celebrating Saeen G M Sayed's birthday in Sukkar. The function was being facilitated by the daughter of a teacher based in Sayadabad, and I was invited to speak after Comrade Hussain Bux. She introduced me in the most unique manner, saying: "Now come, **Chacha** (uncle, father's brother). He is your uncle, he is my uncle, he is uncle to all of us in this patriotic movement for our motherland." This honorific of "uncle" has since become a part of my name—my identity, even. I am called *Chacha* even by my family members, and Fatima by association became known as *Chachi* (aunt) to everyone.

I started my speech with a verse from the poetry of Shah Latif. I then told the gathering that Qadir Magsi had informed me to thank all Sindhi people on his behalf, for demonstrating against his arrest and saving his life. God-willing, I continued, he will be in our midst soon. I challenged the audience to consider the label that had been placed upon us—terrorists—and asserted that it was the time and place for us to decide: Are we terrorists or true patriots? The question demanded an answer. The audience erupted at this provocation to which all Sindhis answered that they were, indeed, true patriots.

In the aftermath of the function, I reflected on the significance of the mass participation of women, which proved that they stood shoulder to shoulder with sons of the soil saving their motherland, Sindh. The credit was due entirely to Gulnaz Laghari and her dedicated team. A senior police official admitted to me that his force had been apprehensive that some incident may take place during the function. There had been no weapons used or exhibited nor slogans raised, however; he congratulated me for the peaceful conclusion of the function.

After some time had passed, Khaki Joyo informed me that some teachers from Mir Khan Laghari wanted to meet me. I stepped down from the dais and met them. They requested a special meeting with me after a formal introduction, to which I responded that I was continuously on the move and in no position to give them any fixed appointment. They expressed their desire to do something for the movement, to which I encouraged them to volunteer for the cause in their own way.

They left, at which point only a number of workers from Sayedabad, and I remained on-site to dismantle the decorations and equipment as well as settle the bills. The materials were duly returned to Karachi by means of a truck. We returned the items borrowed from Mahiran University, too, and after discharging all other obligations I offered my prayers of thanks to the Almighty.

We visited the market in the morning to drink tea. Upon asking the shopkeepers about the tidings of their business, they were happy to share that they had more than three times the usual business on the preceding evening.

Chapter 18

May 29th Women's Protest

Nearly one year after the arrests of Humayoon and Qadir Magsi, the Women's Movement decided to observe the 29th of May as a Black Day—a day of torture. There would be an event, and a lot of effort was put into making it a success. The authorities, meanwhile, were determined to foil our plans.

All roads leading to the city of Hyderabad had been sealed, blocked from movement of any kind on the day of the event. Hyder Chowk was closed by putting up barbed wires and barricades of sand and stone. Buses filled with women that had attempted to enter from Tando Mohammed Khan and Matli were stopped near Fateh Chowk (Cross Road). Buses coming from the villages Bakhsho Laghari, Ghulam Laghari, and Sheikh Bharkyo were not allowed to proceed beyond the Lane Chanel. Those coming from Mirpur Khas and Tando Aliyar were stopped at the Railway Crossing. Women coming from Halla and Sayedabad were not allowed beyond Kaari Mori and they were sent back. The bus carrying the women under the leadership of Dr. Qaram Rustamani from Nawabshah were not allowed to proceed, so they protested.

Their verbal protests escalated into a physical assault, with the police firing weapons. The police injured many demonstrators and killed Fahim Abassi, a first-year student and niece to Dr. Najam Abassi. The police proceeded to take possession of the bus. When news reached a nearby village, Rahul Khan Chang, its residents rushed to the site to provide necessary assistance. The injured who had been left on the road were rushed to hospitals, and others were provided with food and water.

Dodo Mehri was the working president of Taraqi Pasand at the time. He wrote me a letter—it was 1989, so cell phones were not yet available for urgent or rapid communication—declaring, "Uncle: now enough is enough." We could have held a meeting at the crossroads and called off the demonstration, but when I shared the letter with Sister Gulnaz she was furious. She said that I could step away from the movement if I chose, but they would not cancel the protest. I arranged four taxi cabs for sister Gulnaz to travel where she may. An improvised march thus began with people from all parts of the city, including the Kumbhar neighborhood of Bhitainagar, Hirabad, Tando Wali Mohammed, Khhai Road and neighborhood of Talha No. 3. The march was joined by many students and nationalist party workers, and while there were just hundreds of participants at its onset, but the march grew to nearly two or three thousand by the time the procession reached the Wahdat Colony.

The entire procession was monitored by police forces and their allies. At one point a police officer called to me, ordering that we could not advance any further. "You do your duty while we shall do our duty," I curtly replied. This response infuriated the officer. As the procession neared the Indus Hotel, the police resorted to firing tear gas shells and bullets. The son of Khaki Joyo could not be found in the midst of this melee, although he was eventually found and returned to his parents. I was told by Sister Gulnaz and Praha to move away as it was not advisable for any one from central leadership to be arrested. They would face the police on their own, they said.

There happened to be a training college to train junior revenue officers nearby, and in their patriotic zeal they opened the college gates and offered refuge for any protestors. They provided wet clothes to protect against the tear gas.

My sister-in-law fought in an exemplary manner that day. She somehow got hold of a tear gas shell that had not exploded, so she took it in her bare hands and threw it toward the police with all her strength. She burnt her hand in the process.

Fatima, Dodo, Sister Gulnaz, and I went to offer condolences for the death of Gulnaz Fahim Abbasi and stayed with them for three days. We announced then that a mourning ceremony would be held forty days after her death. The ceremony was a solemn occasion, where we all offered prayers and a flower sheet at the tomb. The speech delivered by Dr. Najam Abassi was memorable indeed!

Chapter 19

Anwar's Marriage

Fatima once told me that she wanted to visit Qadir Magsi in jail the next time his family went to visit him. I told her that his family members visit him twice a month, once Nabila Shah and on the other occasion his sister-in-law Shamim. Fatima chose to accompany Shamim, and Shamim readily agreed to Fatima's company.

When Fatima returned from the visit, she had a letter written by Qadir Magsi explaining that it would be quite some time before he would be released. Karim's release would be tied with his and all those who were under detention related to the movement; his would not be considered as a special case. Magsi urged us to go ahead with arranging Anwar's marriage and advised that the ceremony be conducted in such a way as to convey that it was politically affiliated.

We decided that the marriage would be held on December 30th. The invitations were printed and distributed generously to relatives, friends, and political activists. Even the neighborhood landlords were invited. We were not happy, but we had to feign happiness. I told Fatima to make sure that my sister-in-law, Mirzadi, should not be allowed to feel the absence of her son Karim.

The marriage was held during the day at Abbas Bhai Hall, which was quite an impressive venue in those days. Traditional marriage singers who knew Mirzadi came on their own accord and performed. Mirs from Hyderabad, including Mir Ali Ahmed Khan, Mir Nabi Bux and Mir Rafiq son of Mir Rassol Bux, also attended the wedding. It was a big gathering, and special cooks were employed to prepare the food.

It started raining when we returned home, after the marriage ceremonies had been completed. The photographers nevertheless took group photos of various family members. Karim was, of course, detained and thus absent, and Munawar—though free—was not able to attend the ceremony either. Mirzadi and Fatima were anguished by the absence of their sons, so they burst into tears and wails when the hectic marriage ceremony was finished, fearing they might never again see the faces of their beloved sons.

Chapter 20
Incident of Tando Bahawal

In 1992 when Nawaz Sharif was prime minister, he ordered a military operation against antisocial elements. An incident inspired by the order was staged in Tando Bahawal, a village situated 8 kilometers from Hyderabad. The village has many brick kilns, mainly owned by Pathans (residents of Khyber Pakhtunkhwa Province). Many of these Pathans got their sisters and daughters married to local landlords so they could access their wealth. Haji Madad Ali Khan Bhurgri was not only a rich landlord but also a village head; he was married to the sister of one Pathan, Ghulam Muhideen. Haji Madad Ali had no children of his own and was said to be a womanizer.

Ghulam Muhiudeen Khan occupied his sprawling bungalow in Hyderabad and sizable portion of land also as his own property. As general operation by new government was announced, the Pathans took Major Arshad Jamil into confidence and staged an encounter. About 10 persons who were considered an impediment to the execution of their nefarious plan were picked up by military authorities one night and put in a Datsun vehicle. One of them managed to fall from the vehicle and escape, but the remaining nine persons were shot at close range.

Weapons of Indian origin that had come into Major Arshad Jamil's possession were planted on their bodies. Then it was announced that they were Sindhi Nationalist insurgents who had been eliminated in an encounter.

This news was widely shared publicly through media throughout the country, and even the prime minister repeated the claim in the assembly. However, this was exposed as a fake encounter by Fatima, whose party workers recovered the bodies of those killed from Kotri and brought them to Tando Bahawal. Fatima was accompanied by Mirzadi and women from Bakhsho Laghari and other places.

Agitation against these unjust, high-handed murders manifested as protest marches and demonstrations. The tensions escalated when Benazir Bhutto, the leader of the opposition in the parliament, took up the issue. These events were well documented in the issues of the *Herald Magazine*, which contain photos of Fatima and Mirzadi leading the demonstrations.

Major Arshad was eventually arrested, although a number of self-interested and opportunistic elements were working in his favor to impede the justice process. Two daughters of a woman named Jindo immolated themselves at this critical juncture, which resulted in an outcry so intense that it resulted in a conviction and death sentence against Major Arshad.

This was the only instance that an army personnel of the rank of major was hanged at the age of 33. It was indeed a sorry state of affairs that so far no one had been charged for the murder of Surya Badsha or the death of Zulfiqar Ali Bhutto, but let it be remembered that the girls of Tando Bahawal sacrificed themselves to secure justice for their people.

Chapter 21

Sister-in-Law Mirzadi

Mirzadi was born in 1950 to a poor family. Her late father, Dhani Bux, was a cousin of Landlord Haji Jam Khan. Dhani Bux was a known consumer of the local intoxicant, hemp, and was given to fun and frolic. His wife hailed from the village Bago Dodani of Shadadpur, situated in the district of Sanghar, where he used to stay too.

Mirzadi has two sisters and one brother, all of whom were married and settled in Bakhsho Laghari. Mirzadi was the youngest of her siblings but the most courageous among them. She entered our home as a bride in 1968, and my younger brothers got married in 1980; she bore the brunt of the hard work for 12 years. I was very fortunate to have a sister-in-law like her, free from malice or jealously and averse to gossip. She was not too possessive or protective of her children, and she was able to tolerate the admonishment of her children by other family members. Sometimes, tensions arise among the women of a household because of disagreements over the distribution of chores among the family, but Mirzadi did not fall victim to such skirmishes. The traditional conflict and rivalry between daughters-in-law and mothers-in-law were conspicuously absent.

Mirzadi had an amazing capacity to endure hardship. She was prepared to face any situation at any time of day or night, whether it be in the biting cold or the scorching heat. She never hesitated to complete a task expected of her, be it a task for someone younger or older. It did not matter who paid a visit to the house, whether my guest or that of someone else, she would always be prepared to lend a helping hand. I would at times ask her to help me when Fatima was available, but in those moments, she would never ask why I had not solicited the support from my own wife.

Though she was only a sister-in-law to the wives of my two younger brothers, she always treated them as blood sisters. She was more than a match for any man where her capacity for work was concerned, an equal partner in contributing to the prosperity that my family was able to experience.

Women contribute more among a family of farmers. While the men would be busy working in the fields, she would attend to all the household chores. She would cook food for 12 family members and bring it to the fields in the afternoon. She and my brother were estranged from the family for nearly two years, as recounted in an earlier chapter, but I do not blame her for this. That was a result of the machinations of her mother and a sister who poisoned her mind. She felt ashamed for her behavior after-the-fact, and she atoned in her exemplary behavior toward the family.

She never exhibited the slightest sense that Fatima and I loved her children any less than we loved our own. She engaged in laudable work when we moved to Hyderabad too. The entire family recognized this,

Chapter 21: Sister-in-Law Mirzadi

and my younger brothers and their children always treated and respected her as an elder.

I have not hidden anything from my family members. I recognize the anguish that Mirzadi experienced due to the arrest of her son, Karim. In spite of my best efforts, I could not do anything to obtain his release; sometimes I feel guilty on this account. I also realize how painful it must have been as a mother to go empty-handed to meet her son while visiting him periodically in jail. We were all members of one family, and there was no difference or discrimination among my sons Anwar and Munawar and my brothers' sons; even the income and property were shared among us all.

Mirzadi would visit all students who were lodged in jail, bringing their soiled clothes home to wash and return them on her next visit. She would often wash their utensils, too. One day, after cleaning utensils, she was headed to return them at the flat of Abdulah Memon, but while climbing an incline she fell down. She was taken to the hospital but went into a coma as a result of her injuries. She never recovered from that fatal fall and breathed her last on November 27, 1992. May God grant her eternal peace! Her strength of character shall continue to inspire many in the times to come.

Chapter 22
Old Mother

I have spoken of my mother in earlier chapters. She came from a family that could be considered below the poverty line. She inherited asthma as did many in her family. She was the only woman in the family to take care of the household with three younger brothers-in-law, without the luxury of exercising any choice; she was needed to work whether she was well or sick. The male members of the household would leave early in the morning to labor in the fields, which meant she was alone at home to face the daily challenges and wait for their return in the evenings. She told us that in her day, even the flour needed to be ground by hand in a stone mill. She would stitch clothes herself, using only needle and thread. To add a layer of complexity, cloth and food were rationed by the government at that time and could only be obtained from designated shops.

My mother bore nine children at home, assisted by some local midwife or kind woman of the neighborhood. She was devoted to her family and avoided the village gossip, leading the family on the same path of subsistence and barely existing. With the passage of time, she had daughters-in-law added to the family, all obedient and respectful.

My mother was happy in her old age that she could rest well, and her daughters-in-law could take care of the household chores. She always remembered that, at her urging, I purchased a bus for my brother and sustained a serious loss.

My father did his best in his lifetime too. I am who I am today as a result of their blessings alone. I suffer from a sense of guilt that I did not devote my time to my parents in adequate measure. Perhaps I have devoted more time to my social and political activities to attain fame and praise that is in its nature temporary. I sometimes ponder over the time spent on these activities, reflecting on the time that I stole from my dear parents and family members.

My mother endured illness for a long time. In her last days, my mother would insist that she did not need my money for treatment: "I need *you* to be with me." I would tell her that she was often ill, but her condition would always improve with the proper medications. "I have an important engagement to meet," she would say. "Son, do as you wish and be quiet."

When I was busy at a function, I received a message that my mother had passed away. Mother: Today, I genuinely regret that I did not give you the time that was due to you and instead spent time on irrelevant activities.

May God grant her eternal peace!

Chapter 23
Saleh Junejo

Saleh Junejo used to work at the Sangahr sugar mills, but his employment was terminated after some dispute. Junejo appealed to the labor court for compensation; through Anwar's connections to the offices of Zain Shah, Junejo was awarded a compensation of 150,000 rupees.

When Abrar Qazi's brother, Amitaz Qazi, later became a commissioner, he started to harass Junejo by leveling false charges against him. He would be sent to various police stations all the time. His wife and mother came to meet Fatima one day at our residence at Nassem Apartments. They apprised her of their plight, revealing that they had been searching for him at every police station; they would hear that he was being held at the Dighri police station, but others would say that he was being held at the Mithi police station. The search was proving unsuccessful—party officials claimed that they did not even know for certain if he had been detained.

The women asked Fatima for her assistance, expressing that even if they could not secure his release, they were determined to discover where Saleh Junejo was being detained and on what charges. Fatima expressed that she was but an illiterate woman from a small village, yet instead of forsaking the women, she supported them in their quest.

I conveyed to Fatima that I believed the situation presented to be exceedingly complex, and I even attempted to dissuade her as she was a complete stranger to the various places they may have to visit. I ultimately advised her to bring enough cash for her journey and to be careful of pickpockets.

Fatima thus traveled with Mohammed Saleh's family by rickshaw to the bus stand where the bus would take them to Mithi. When they reached the Mithi police station, they were redirected to speak with Salem Kot, to which end they traveled first to Diplo and were eventually directed to Nagar Parkar. They realized, after boarding the bus headed to Nagar Parkar, that they would not reach their destination in time and thus returned to Mithi around 11:30 p.m.

They inquired there about one Mr. Nanadlal but were told that there were many persons by that name. It was not until Fatima revealed that he was a comrade associated with the movement led by Qadir Magsi that they were eventually escorted to his house. It was one o'clock in the morning when they reached his house. Fatima introduced herself and her companions, all of whom were invited to rest in his home. They decided that they should leave for Hyderabad by the first available train and were subsequently informed that the first Coaster Bus to Hyderabad would depart at four o'clock in the morning. Their generous hosts agreed to lead them to the bus stop at that time. Fatima and her companions were extremely tired and exhausted when they reached Hyderabad, so I convinced the women to rest for the day in our home.

Chapter 23: Saleh Junejo

Dr. Hamid Memon and Anwar were classmates and good friends, even related through their in-laws. In the wake of the incident on September 30th, Dr. Memon left his wife at our place and told her that we were her parents as well as in-laws. Dr. Memon was eventually incarcerated in Karachi, and after some time, Fatima accompanied his wife to visit him. There was a sudden downpour during their journey, however, and the streets were quickly flooded. Traffic and movement of any kind ground to a halt and, amidst the panic, Fatima and her traveling companion lost track of the road they needed to follow.

They sought refuge in the home of a kind person who not only provided them with a separate room to stay but provided them with garments so that their clothes, which had been soaked, could be left to dry. The kind man shared dinner as well as breakfast with them and, when their garments had dried the next morning, he hailed a taxi and saw them comfortably to Hyderabad. Dr. Memon's family endured five years of difficulty before he was released.

Fatima did not do any of this to obligate anyone to her; on the contrary, Fatima's selfless service speaks to her dedication and devotion to the cause, which filled her with immense satisfaction.

Chapter 24

Fatima's Attitude toward Activists

Fatima was quite oblivious to the nature and purpose of the movement to which she had dedicated herself. She was never educated about the history of freedom movements or their national heroes, and she did bother herself with high political slogans or care to attach meaning to them. Fatima was the manifestation of tender love and affection; she took it upon herself to care for anyone she came in contact with, certain only that anyone who came to her were Sindhi children—most from poor families—who were precious to their mothers. This alone entitled them to her selfless service, and she dedicated herself to serve them without distinction. A number of leaders within the movement would express their gratitude to Fatima, expressing that they would respect her as if she were their own mother until the end of time. There were others who would forget about Fatima's service, but so long as she had done all she could and fulfilled what she felt was her duty, this did not bother her. She served all those engaged in the movement from 1972 to 2008.

As the "Aunt" of the movement, Fatima's home functioned as a headquarters for the movement. While our Nassem Apartments flat consisted of only two rooms, it was sufficient enough to hold a central committee meeting for the Party. Members of the committee, sans Qadir Magsi, would gather there in the morning for business and spend the afternoon relaxing. The door was open, and all would be served tea or provided with sufficient quantities of food when hungry.

I recall one morning when Faqir Deen Mohammed, Ashiq Solangi, Saleh Junejo, and Nandlal Malhi were all present and busy in our home: Some were reading, some were writing, and others were deep in conversation. Fatima prepared breakfast for all and was about to serve them but, in that moment, she felt dizzy and fell to the floor. Fatima hit her head on the gas cooker and was rendered unconscious. Everyone rushed to help her. She regained consciousness when Faqir Deen Mohammed Kumbhar sprinkled water on her face. They insisted that she rest and forget about serving breakfast, but Fatima insisted that she would boil eggs to feed her guests. They should not even think of leaving their aunt's home without eating breakfast! They were allowed to disperse only after they were fed.

There was a time when Mehboob Abro was wanted by the police. Police Officer Hamid Thahim rushed into our home one day with backup and arrested Abro, who was escorted out with little resistance. All the politically affiliated people who were in our home at the time quickly left, until only a few family members remained. This was prudent, for a posse of policemen returned just half an hour later to search for "infidels." Fatima's nephew who was just 17 or 18 years of age, was identified by the police. Fatima vehemently protested, insisting that none in the home were *dacoit* or ran any illegal activity such as

Chapter 24: Fatima's Attitude toward Activists

drinking or gambling. She asked the officer if he were not ashamed for behaving in such an undignified manner and admonished him by asserting that he should treat her with respect given that she was his mother's age. The infuriated officer pushed her, causing Fatima to hit her head against the wall and fall unconscious.

Media and press representatives reached the home at this point and took Fatima's photo. The photo and information about the incident were published and widely distributed the next day in the newspapers. The police reluctantly released Rassol Bux after 15 days.

In 1998 the Sindh Taraqi Pasand Party (STP) decided to plan a long march from Sukkar to the governor's house in Karachi. The event required extensive preparation until the day finally arrived. We celebrated Motherland Day at the clock tower in Sukkar before the march to Karachi commenced. The central leadership went underground for tactical reasons after the first stretch of the march had been completed and the decision was made to give the call to the rank and file for a Total Strike on March 26th instead of completing the march. The workers, however, were not prepared to abandon the march; they insisted that Dr. Dodo continue to lead the march and, after significant reluctance, Dr. Dodo agreed to the wishes of the party's rank and file membership. The entire leadership ostensibly supported the decision by the time the marchers reached Moro.

Participants in the march were fed and looked after by poor workers Abbas Banglani and Qamar Burro in Sakrand, but we received ghastly news as we proceeded from Saeedabad to Hala: A bomb blast in a bus moving from Nawabshah had killed more than seven Sindhi passengers. Relatives of the dead collected the corpses of their loved ones the next day (which happened to be Eid day, a Holy day of celebration). The irony was magnified when the poor workers who had fed us in Sakrand and Sabu Rahu were framed and arrested for the dastardly deed. Abbas Banglani and Qamar Burro Fatima were greatly distressed to hear the news upon their arrest. This news was conveyed to me by some friends who came to meet me during the long march.

We had decided before the march commenced that at least ten people would undertake the entire march along its route, but we only secured seven volunteers to commit to the arduous task. We decided to spend Eid day at Bhit Shah in the village of Shah Latif; family members of those people who were walking continuously would come to meet them there. Fatima showed up with all of her female family members, bringing enough food for more than 25 people. She sat with the volunteers from the march and boosted their morale, urging them to take up the cause to release those who had been arrested and to mourn the deaths of those who had died in the tragic incident at Sukrand.

Fatima continued to Hyerdabad and organized women there to welcome the marchers at their next major stop, Hyder Chowk. The considerable crowd, which gathered on that day, bore testimony to Fatima's hard work and organizing prowess. Fatima delivered the first public speech of her life at this gathering, and Dodo delivered an impressive speech too. Fatima guaranteed that a large gathering of women was present when we finally reached the governor's home in Karachi; she arrived that day with *ten* buses filled with women volunteers.

Fatima and I returned home after the long march. I had become exhausted because of the heat, and Fatima was not well. We lived alone at this point of our lives. Munawar had been living at Nassem Apartments

Chapter 24: Fatima's Attitude toward Activists

in Qasimabad since 1988, and Anwar lived separately because wherever we lived became a base for political activities. We felt as though, in the long run, this dynamic would not be beneficial for Anwar.

Once, party workers from Jacobabad—a full wagon of women and five to seven male workers—descended on our home for Motherland Day. This was arranged by Jameela Soomro, Rubina Kalhoro, and Intzar Chhalgari's sister. They all rested and decided to leave their luggage in our home before departing for the venue of the function. When they returned from the event and prepared to load their belongings into the van, the driver of the vehicle decided it would be prudent to turn the van around in a vacant lot near our residence (where VIP flats have since been constructed) instead of maneuvering in a tight space. The move was intended to save time, but the wet earth was loose, and the van got stuck in the mud. The van could not be lifted despite our best efforts. Party leaders who had been at our home could have helped care for those stranded, but they had already departed for their homes that night, so it was up to us to face the unfortunate situation. I went out to purchase necessary materials to look after our influx of guests, and Fatima spent the night with 60 women in one room. We tried everything to lift the van, from using tractors to calling the Transport Company who had provided the van (they were busy running other routes). We eventually hired workers from Halani Corner who had heavy jacks; we exerted ourselves from four o'clock that morning until eleven o'clock the next evening before the van was finally freed.

The travelers all thanked us for our trouble as they left, but none ever cared to inform us as to whether they reached their destinations safely. Such is the way of the world!

Chapter 25
Chachi of Sindh Falls Sick

Fatima had not been keeping well since 2000. We have a number of children and relatives, however, who were by then successful and always present to support her. Anwar became a practicing doctor, independent from us, whereas Munawar remains an engineer living as an exile in a foreign country. My nephew, Ghulam Raza, a son of my brother Ganhwar Khan and whom we fondly call Gul, stayed with us. He is named after my father, and I love him as if he were my own son. Though he is not old, he has matured through his life experiences. We had a mutually beneficial agreement: Fatima and I look after him and his education and, in turn, he looks after our health. I brought my brother's eldest daughter, Nasreen, into our home as well; Fatima and I believed it was our responsibility to look after the well-being and education of all their children, especially considering the extent to which they suffered for me—and all the police station doors they knocked on for me—as a result of my political activities. Nasreen was raised by my sister-in-law Mirzadi, who did not have any blood daughters of her own, and she has since been admitted into Mira School for further education. She stays with her cousins, Amir and Karim.

In those days Gul would hasten to the doctors and bring us medicines at the slightest discomforts that accompanied our advancing age. If he felt that he could not handle a situation, he would reach out to his cousins, Dr. Anwar, Amir, and Karim. Fatima complained to Gul about her discomfort one day. Her blood pressure continued to be on the lower side, to which Gul would often give her salt and sweet water. Her body appeared to be very cold that day, however, and he got in touch with Karim; Karim immediately sent his nephew Majeed with instructions to bring Fatima to Rajputana Hospital before Majeed rushed to book a room there. He deposited 5,000 rupees and reserved the room. I stayed with her in the hospital for about a week, after which she was discharged, and we returned home. I was suffering from asthmatic attacks myself in those days, yet somehow we pulled along.

The Progressive Party cancelled the membership of Munawar and Dr. Dodo in 2000. Fatima and I decided to leave the party too. We were anguished, thinking that our sacrifices over 16 years had come to naught. We felt that we had been cheated, but we also felt that we were guilty of contributing to illusions and delusions among the Sindhi masses. We remained satisfied, at least, that we had remained clean and not indulged in any wrongdoing where our personal lives were concerned. Yes! Let me confess we did make some wrong decisions. God will forgive us for our genuine mistakes. Many more left the party after our exit.

There was an abhorrent attempt on the life of Dr. Rahim Solangi at this time, an act which was condemned by everyone in Sindh. After some time in the face of continued injustice, we constituted a Sindh National Council Forum with a few friends; although its scale was limited, we had the silent cooperation of many clean people in society

Chapter 25: Chachi of Sindh Falls Sick

during this venture. In the month of March, we wanted to observe an international day of protests against the construction of big dams, so we called a press conference to announce that the Council would march from Sessions Court to the Hyderabad Press Club. When the day of the protest arrived, Fatima had mobilized more than 100 women protestors to be present. We had cooperation of good friends to make this protest successful. Among them were Dr. Ashwathama, Abdul Fatah Daudpoto, Majid Soomro, Akram Soomro, and others from Hyderabad. With the help of these friends, new trends were introduced in the Sindhi Nationalist Movement at Karachi and Larkana.

We would meet and honor many visitors to Sindh from abroad, apprising them of the realities of exploitation, which led to an extreme sense of alienation of the Sindhi masses from the state of Pakistan and a desire for freedom. Mr. Landry once visited from the United States; we hosted him and took him to many iconic places, including Sindh University, Bhit Shah, and Keenjhar Lake. We discussed political conditions in the state of Pakistan, which no doubt perturbed the intelligence agencies, but that did not matter to him. We escorted him to his hotel that night after sightseeing and returned for breakfast the next morning. Rahim and I arrived after comrade Hussain Bux, who complained that he did not get proper sleep. We became suspicious that he may have been in danger, but that was not the case. He expressed his concern, instead, that Fatima would pass before she was able to see her son Munawar.

Dr. Rahim told comrade Hussain Bux that we had tried to obtain visas to the United States several times, but each application had been rejected. We told him the last time we had applied was 2002, to which he recommended we try once again and send him copies of the papers. He would take care of the rest.

Fatima's health and my own soon gave way, and thus we retired completely from active politics.

Chapter 26

My Brother's Death

It was a calm night in January when someone suddenly knocked on our door. I prayed to God that nothing was amiss. I found my grandson, Karim Laghari, standing in the night; he told me that his maternal grandfather was seriously ill from an acute stomachache. I immediately rushed with him to Civil Hospital. There were no responsible doctors or employees working that night; instead of admitting my brother, they gave him a number of pills with instructions to return the next morning. We returned to our flat in Saddar.

I asked Karim to help his grandfather ascend the steep incline to our flat, since my home was at the top of the building. While I have always known my brother to withstand any pain, when I approached him with breakfast in the morning I found him suffering from acute pain. His sons, Karim and Rassol Bux, informed me that they had been in touch with Dr. Aziz Laghari, who had set an appointment for eleven o'clock that morning to perform a surgery. Nearly half of my brother's intestines were removed, a procedure from which it was exceedingly difficult for any patient to survive. My son, Anwar, warned us that he would survive perhaps only six months from the operation. Karim and

Rassol Bux were very worried about their father, as was I. I dutifully stayed with him every day from nine in the morning to eleven at night. He had no control over his physical functions, so he often soiled his clothes. I sent them to be laundered and helped him don fresh robes a number of times each day.

Karim's maternal cousin, Amir, was set to marry within four or five days at that point, and the Eid holidays were approaching. I sensed that my brother preferred to be at home at our Saddar flat. He affirmed this suspicion when asked and, when I warned him that it may be difficult for him to climb the stairs to the fourth floor, he assured me that he could manage. I told Amir and Karim to transport him to the flat before they attended to the marriage ceremonies. My sister Marium Laghari also came to our flat to assist her brother.

The marriage was set to take place in Karachi with the reception arranged at our village, Bakhsho Laghari. Fatima attended the marriage in Karachi but, upon returning home and seeing the state of my brother, decided to forgo the village reception. Fatima stood by my side to help me– we were a great team. She would wash my brother's soiled clothes without hesitation. I gave him massages for temporary comfort. He would say that I was acting like his father and did not need to be doing all that I was, but I would have none of it. My brother was transported back to the hospital when the boys returned from the wedding, then eventually discharged and returned to our flat in Saddar. At this point his sons suggested that they move him to his own house, to which he replied that this, too, was his own house. Gul volunteered to accompany him to his house in Qasimabad, which he consented to as his health began to improve.

Chapter 26: My Brother's Death

He then experienced a relapse in his abdominal pains, however, and was once again admitted to Rajputana Hospital. As his health continued to deteriorate, he begged my forgiveness for any wrongs he may have committed. He breathed his last at 11:00 p.m. on June 9, 2004. May God grant him eternal peace.

Brothers are brothers; they are meant to love and praise one another. I deem myself lucky to have had such a brother. At this juncture between life and death, however, one must stoically accept His will.

Chapter 27

To America for Fatima's Treatment

Munawar called me in January 2008 to say that I would be receiving papers from the immigration department and, should I abide by the requirements and submit them to the proper authorities, I may be able to secure passage to the United States. Fatima's health was declining each day, and she was distraught that my efforts would prove futile. I was determined. I collected the necessary papers and documents in due course and completed all that I could. The American embassy finally called us for a personal interview on April 24, 2008, only requiring that we produce an official medical report to support our claims before our meeting the next week. Fatima's condition continued to worsen as I was busy collecting necessary documents, and at one point she was admitted to the Agha Khan Hospital in Karachi. Anwar was, thankfully, allowed to stay with his mother.

When she was released from the hospital we traveled to the embassy in Islamabad. I told Fatima that, by the grace of God and with the help of Dr. Ismail, all the required papers had been obtained. We stayed at the home of Zardari Ghulam Hyder in Islamabad, who served us well and looked after us as their own; in response to their graceful hospitality, we blessed them and their children. Mrs. Zardari brought us to the American Embassy in the morning. When Anwar was not allowed to accompany us into the interview, I assured him that he had no cause to worry and that we were capable of navigating the situation ourselves. I had confirmed that all our paperwork was in order and had even prepared myself by practicing answers to questions that I expected. I would not voluntarily offer anything to the authorities, as instructed by Munawar, and would thus confine myself to only address the questions asked. Munawar also told me to carry 800 USD along with me, as it was possible they would ask for my deposit fee on the spot. Our names were called after about an hour, and we navigated a number of entrances before reaching the appropriate counter. Once they had secured our affidavits and taken our passports, they congratulated us and said that our passports would be stamped and shipped back to our address in Hyderabad within a week or two.

I found Anwar was anxiously waiting for us when we emerged. I told him that we had been granted the visa to travel to the United States, to which Munawar expressed apprehension over the phone. He predicted that, because we had not deposited any amount, our passports would be returned to us by mail without any stamps. Anwar reassured Munawar that all would be well. We were set to return to Zardari's residence, though a friend of mine from Rawalpindi, DCO Jamal Mustafa Sayed, wanted us to go stay with him. We agreed to have dinner with him that evening, at his insistence. The dinner was delicious, though for her health Fatima was not able to eat much. We returned to Zardari's residence that night to retrieve our luggage and prepare for the flight

Chapter 27: To America for Fatima's Treatment

to Karachi the next morning. We departed the next day and, from Karachi, reached our home in Hyderabad by taxi.

I received the call on Saturday morning that our passports had been delivered. We informed Munawar of the development, to which he wanted us to depart as soon as possible; he was alarmed at the state of his mother's health. Munawar tried to convince a number of his friends to accompany us on the journey to the United States, but those plans did not materialize. I told Munawar not to worry, ensuring him that we would reach him on our own. I soon booked the tickets and, though I was concerned about Fatima's health, I maintained a consistent line of prayer to God and made all necessary arrangements to depart. Many people appeared at our home to see us off and share their well-wishes. The house was packed all night, until we left early the next morning! Fatima was not well, but at the same time everyone was too excited that she would be reunited with her dear son after 15 years of staying away.

I arranged for a wheelchair for Fatima at the airport. The flight to Washington, DC, was successful. I secured help from an African American man for two hundred rupees, and he not only gave us a wheelchair but escorted us to the Immigration Counter. All our papers were checked, our palm impressions were taken, and we produced the letter that we had received from Islamabad when prompted. We were allowed to pass. We retrieved our bags from the conveyer and emerged from the airport. I could not immediately spot Munawar, though he was already there. We asked the man helping us navigate the airport to call him and, within two minutes, he was standing before us. Munawar tipped the employee and then fell at the feet of his mother. It was a reunion between a mother and son to behold, indeed! Munawar told

Najam to wait with us as he drove his car to meet us, and we were soon on our way to our son's home in the United States. We had made it. Munawar regaled his mother with many stories to keep her in good humor on the drive. He wanted to know her favorite dish so that he may purchase it for her. Fatima only beamed in satisfaction, overjoyed by the reunion.

Though we already had stocks of medicine from the Agha Khan Hospital of Karachi, Munawar set about contacting various friends and doctors in the United States. He set an appointment for us the next morning, at which point we were taken to the office of an organization known as TASSC. This group supports people who have been victims of state persecution; Munawar is one of the founding member of the organization. The organization started with only five people and later grew to more than 500 members. Members of TASSC were taken aback and became very concerned when they observed Fatima's condition. They tried to arrange for our breakfast, but we politely declined, explaining that we had already eaten before arriving. They insisted on at least sharing tea with us, an offer which we accepted. They wanted to host a dinner in our honor, too, at which point Munawar assured them that we would be in town for a while yet and would at some point accept their gracious hospitality. Members of TASSC immediately set about creating an appointment for us to meet with an insurance company, urging them to expedite the process for the parents of a founding member.

We traveled to the insurance company's office and, within an hour, we were admitted. The doctor at the establishment who checked Fatima took a special interest in her medical condition, calling a security officer to take the case on an urgent basis. We went to a massive, secure

Chapter 27: To America for Fatima's Treatment

hospital after the initial checkup, where Fatima was immediately admitted. Fatima had to undergo many tests before any treatment could start, including a removal of the water in her abdomen. The hospital offered no facilities for relatives or friends to stay with patients, so we exchanged cell phone numbers with the health care professionals and stayed in the waiting room. Munawar suggested that I settle in at his place after a long time of waiting, assuring me that he would stay with a friend near the hospital for the night in case there was any need. I spent the next day at his home, where Munawar brought his mother at eleven o'clock that evening.

He relayed to me that the water in her abdomen had been removed, and we would receive the results within a day or two. The preliminary reports were not promising. I do not know English and, beyond this, am not familiar with medical terminology; for this reason, I was prone to accept anything that was told to me. We continued to medicate Fatima about a week, as instructed, at which point she was readmitted to the hospital to repeat the procedure. All our efforts did not bear the desired results.

Munawar's friend, Dr. Shyamlal, a renowned oncologist from the city of Daharki in the Ghotki district of Sindh, had been communicating with Munawar daily about the reports and medication. He was living in Atlanta at the time and urged Munawar to bring his mother to the hospital where he was working, promising that a team of doctors would be able to care for Fatima. We consented. The flight took about two hours, and we found Dr. Shyamlal waiting for us at the airport. We stayed at his home that night, and the next morning Fatima was transported to his hospital. We were in Atlanta for about a week, and I could make out from their conversations that Fatima had only a number of days to live. Death must eventually come to all humans—no one is immortal! They told Munawar to fulfill every wish of his mother in her final days; no restrictions with regard to food or anything else should be placed upon her. Munawar was advised to send his parents back to Sindh as soon as possible.

Munawar was inconsolable upon hearing that the worst possibility was coming to fruition. Fatima, for her part, was satisfied; all that she had yearned for was to see her son once more before her departure from this world, and that wish had been fulfilled. I had helped bring this gift to her, she would tell me. Fatima did lament that she had not been allowed to visit her son when she was able-bodied, but she was grateful nonetheless that the will of God had transpired as it had.

Many Sindhis have settled in the United States, and many wanted to play host when they learned that we were in the country. We had to decline all such invitations, due to the circumstances. Munawar was constantly in touch with his brother, Anwar, and apprised him of the situation. We all worked together to convince Fatima that she should return to Sindh. I told her that we had come to the United States primarily for treatment, but that the same medicines could be taken at our home in Hyderabad. Anwar and his son, Assad, were insistent, too, saying that with our newly acquired visas we would be able to return to the United States whenever we desired. She would say, "Have we come all this way to return?" whenever the subject of return was broached, though in her last days she would often say that she should return, for she missed her grandson Assad a lot. It took Munawar one week to convince his mother.

Chapter 27: To America for Fatima's Treatment

We had reached the United States on May 1st and left on May 30th. Munawar accompanied us on the flight as far as Dubai, at which point he could not travel further. We reached Karachi airport at six o'clock in the morning on June 2nd. All our relatives were anxiously waiting for us upon our arrival, and they had requested a number of expeditious formalities of the airport officials so that we could emerge on a priority basis. I lodged a complaint that one of my bags had not arrived from Dubai, providing our Hyderabad address where the bag was to be sent. While all our relatives were happy upon our return, they were simultaneously concerned over the health of their "aunt." Fatima stayed with me on the ground floor until June 22nd, when Anwar insisted that he take her to his home. Fatima told him that this was not necessary, for they were at a stage in their life when they were all working and needed proper rest. Alas, any strength to climb the stairs had left her. Anwar picked her up on June 23rd and brought her to his home, where her health became increasingly precarious with each passing day. There, in addition to our other relatives, my sister and her nieces were all available to help.

Fatima told her grandson, Assad, that she wanted to speak with Munawar by phone on June 26th. He immediately and repeatedly tried to get in touch with him, but Assad could not reach Munawar due to poor connectivity. Around nine o'clock that evening, there was a call from Munawar, but by then, Fatima had lost the capacity to hear anything or even to speak. The irony! Munawar frantically wished to speak to her and hear her voice, but she could not hear him. These are the unspeakable cruelties that life heaps upon us!

The girls of the house insisted that I get some rest, promising that they would keep vigil. It was four o'clock in the morning, and I agreed to the proposal. I returned at ten that morning. Anwar had left the home to procure groceries, and Amir's wife and the girls of the house were busy reciting the Holy Quran for the salvation of Fatima, so that she may find everlasting peace in heaven. I told the girls that it was their turn to rest, and I resumed watch over my dearest Fatima. I asked her about her health, to which she half opened her eyes. When I asked if she would like any water, she opened her eyes again. I gave her two spoons filled with water, keeping the spoon on her lips. When I tried a third time, my nephew, Amir, told me that I should not give her any more water. I kept the spoon and water jug on the table. I took out a tissue paper to wipe her lips, but before I could touch her lips with the tissue, Fatima had surrendered herself to God. It was 10:35 a.m. on June 27, 2008.

Fatima had valiantly fought death, but at last she lost the battle. May God grant her eternal refuge.

There were countless relatives, friends, and well-wishers across Sindh supporting Fatima throughout her illness. I will make a special mention of Dr. Manzoor Memon, who from January to June in that final year did not miss a day coming to visit her and inquire about her health. I cannot name them all, but I wish to express my deepest gratitude to them for their moral support in this period of crisis.

Chapter 28

My Mother: Reflections by Munawar

Mother you are gone! I cannot believe it. You are always with me, in my memories, with your advice, your smiles and your tears. The touch of your hands, your fond kisses, your courage, your uprightness … all the lessons you taught me.

"Always look after poor."

"Son, my blessings are with you always! No harm ever would come to you. You will live like a King. You will never be short of anything. You will roll in gold and diamonds. Remember my words!"

Mother, you blessed me with these words until the end of your life.

She used to shower these blessings in her Seraiki dialect, with full confidence and love. I knew that this bad news was to come any day. Her insistence that she wished to speak with me on her last day is the ultimate reflection of our lovely relationship between mother and son.

It is only love that matters in this life. This life is, after all, but a transitory existence. Everyone has to leave, though one does not know the time and place of their departure. I could sense in her last two days that she was to fall silent and that I was never to hear her voice again.

Mother! We are not separate. I am with you, and you are with me all the time. I feel it. The United Nations observes June 26th as Survivors Day, and you survived that day and you left us on June 27th.

Death is inevitable. It is bound to come for everyone one day. This world is beset with many problems that are the destiny of man to solve: life, death, religion, and science. I have pondered over all these subjects for quite a while. I have been thinking of these subjects before and after the death of my mother. My thinking has been influenced by many, but the most important influence remains the great poet Shah Latif "Bhitai."

My mother, in spite of her ill health, traveled ten thousand miles across the seas and stayed with me for a month. We had many meaningful and memorable conversations during that month which I will always cherish. I only wish that she had been healthy so that I could have taken her to all the places where I had resided and spent the days of my life, sharing a part of my life with her. Alas, her health was not good, and I could not share all that I wished with her.

To this day I am awestruck by her courage and capacity to face adversity and the challenges of life! During the one month she spent with me, she reinforced my faith in the superior strength of the female gender. All this helped me to understand female characters portrayed by Shah Latif in a clearer perspective.

Chapter 28: My Mother: Reflections by Munawar

I had never seen before my own eyes the struggle between life and death so vividly.

I believe that, apart from the lack of education or opportunities, it is the suppression of women through the ages that has caused great harm to our society. Our entire society has been rendered crippled by this unequal condition. The very question about the character and strength of a woman is redundant. Latif has rightly said:

"Let us ask Sohini who knows how to love."

It is the emotion of love that endows us with the greatest strength. Sheikh Ayaz (an eminent Sindhi poet) has also written: "It is love that invests us with greatest strength." This really calls for great sacrifice!

Death, life, love, pain, and pleasure… the relationships between father and brothers are all fine, but the relationship of a mother is something unique. In this relationship, the character of a woman assumes unprecedented heights. A mother is a person's first school. This institution is not dependent on any prior training, budget, or any staff. One does not require any prerequisite to enter this school. This institution of motherhood needs to be properly understood. In our society it is taken for granted but it needs to be valued for its contribution to human civilization and culture. Then, a question looms; if a child is devoid of a mother… in that case what would happen?

Mothers are, in fact, the manifestations of a God on earth! It is for this reason that whatever I learned from my mother I need to ponder deeply. Death is a phenomena that connects us to science, religion, nature, and the concept of the Almighty. I had many discussions with

K. R. Malkani about this; he opined that it is at the juncture of death that religion becomes necessary.

There is an anecdote. It is said, during the times of Buddha, there was an incident when a mother was distraught at the death of her child and appealed to him to give life to the child. Buddha told her to bring a handful of grain from the house of a person where no death had ever occurred. She went around the entire town and, at last, came empty-handed to Buddha. He consoled her by saying all the life that comes into existence must exit. This is the law of nature, and we all are subject to that supreme law. All prophets, greats, poets, and philosophers had to exit. Dust, after all, has to return to dust. Therefore Shah Latif says:

> *"All night those who remerged beloved*
> *Abdul Latif says their dust also evoked respect*
> *Millions come and bow before them"*

We have to respect this dust, the soil. Those who ceaselessly serve her will gain respect. All greats had to physically leave this mortal coil. Some say that they still live, that we are able to see and touch them. Some believe that they continue their watch over us. I have experienced these sensations. I always feel that my mother has moved only from one room to another, and I am constantly under her watch.

She was loving as well as strict. She would scold me while simultaneously showering me with love. She could never remain angry for a long time and could be easily persuaded. She understood the real meaning of tears and laughter, pain and pleasure. She was proud of being a worker and would often say that God is always a friend of those who work. She was a loving mother as well as a sister, wife, and friend.

Chapter 28: My Mother: Reflections by Munawar

She faced troubles and tribulations in her life, but she always said that she was amply rewarded for her troubles. She was grown up a mature lady, yet she maintained a childlike innocence. In the national political movement, she would render her advice and work like a common cadre. As one friend put it, she was like a character from Gorky's *Mother*. She was devoted to the great poet Shah Latif Bhitai and understood the deeper meanings of his poetry. Her advice to me was that "Risalo of Shah Latif" will remain as your education as well as your soul. It is his poetry that will brighten the path for Sindh. He is your Master as well as your Protector.

She played a significant role in giving shelter to underground leaders and workers of the Sindhi Nationalist Movement. She would often nurse them when they were injured or bedridden. She was also a melodious singer who sang to me many traditional songs, mostly songs by Shah Latif.

She herself was not educated but she was great supporter of women's' education. She was very strict about our education. She would often jokingly say that she had remained the principal of the institute that we went to.

Her separation is unbearable indeed! The state of Pakistan has deprived me of many things, and now it has snatched my dear mother too. She is away from me in her physical form, but she is always with me through her guidance. She is with me in my thoughts, thus guiding my life. I will always remember her instruction, "Look after the poor my son!"

May God give me strength to live up to her expectation!

Fatima of Sindh

Long live mother, long live Latif
Jiye Sind! Huq Moujood! * (Let Truth Prevail)

* Truth is all-pervasive and eternal.

Chapter 29

Remembering My Mother by Anwar

The mourning period over Mother's death ended on Friday, July 4, 2008.

Life resumed its usual rhythm, and everything appeared to be as it had always been. In fact, the bond between a mother and her child is so unique that there is no less than a flood of memories when I think of her. But what can I write?! Only a few memories etched in my mind! I carry her in my heart, and her memories course through the blood in my veins. This relationship cannot be defined by words alone; I become tearful whenever I think of her! Remembering her affection, love and care … I feel helpless to express myself.

During our childhood she would bathe us, dress us properly, and apply a black spot to ward off any evil eye that may befall us. She would always pray, "God look after the well-being of children throughout the world and, thereby, look after my children too."

I remember there was a childhood game between boys that required holding our breath (*KODI KODI*). After playing the game, I returned with my uncle who was gleefully swinging his cane. He inadvertently hit me near the eye with his cane, and I began to bleed profusely. My mother reached to hold me in her tight embrace upon seeing the blood on me, then after treating me she put me on her lap and sang me to sleep with a lullaby. Later in life, I tried to put my own children to sleep singing that lullaby … I felt that the magic of my mother was missing from it.

Mother was born in a poor home. Though her maternal grandparents were quite well off, her paternal grandparents were poor. She was orphaned at a very young age, after which she was brought up as an orphan in her maternal grandparents' house. She was ignored while her cousins were sent to school, and she did not receive the benefit of any education. Her being uneducated made her conscious about the importance of the education. She realized early in life that the only way to progress, lies in education. It is the key. Though I tended to be truant in childhood, she was very strict with me about my education. She used to encourage me by saying, "We do not have any wealth, but education is the only wealth that no one can steal from us. It cannot be traded, but it will give you enough courage and knowledge to surmount any difficulty in life."

She used to work in the fields with other members of the family to make both ends meet. She was a good worker and was in demand at other fields. Her income would supplement our educational needs for books and stationary supplies.

In consultation and with the help of Mother, I was able to go for higher education to Hyderabad and stay with her cousins. At that time we were not in a position to have our own house in Hyderabad. She would visit us whenever she could afford. I stayed with her cousins and studied up to matriculation in that house.

At this juncture Mother desired to have her own house in Hyderabad so that she would be able to educate her sons and be with them. We rented a one-room tenement at Liaqat Colony in Hyderabad. As our relatives had helped us for further education, she repaid that debt by looking after the education of children of the entire joint family. As stated earlier she was very particular and strict about the education of all the children under her care. In intermediate examination, I got good marks and was able to secure admission into a medical college. I could progress further due to hard and diligent efforts. By this time Munawar had started going to Mehran College. At this point Mother thought that the days of her hardship would soon end. Let me say here that all those children of the family who grew up studying under the hawks-eye of Mother now occupy important positions. Some are doctors, others are engineers, and still more are bank officers.

There was a sort of political upheaval when we reached the university level. Youth across Sindh subscribed to the ideology of Sindhi Nationalism to preserve a separate Sindhi identity. The atrocities committed by the military under the rule of martial law fueled the fire. The youth of Sindh stood up to face the challenge, and we were sucked into this wave. Mother always stood by us and the downtrodden, and she would encourage us in such activities. Many coworkers would come our home and be provided with food and treated as family members. She would be present even during our strategic discussions.

As the movement grew in strength, the government planted their agent provocateurs in the movement and tried to split the movement. This is the old strategy of the rulers. During 1983–1986, students were divided to such an extent that inter-student conflicts were staged. Many students lost their lives as a result.

Two groups at the University of Sindh were incited to fight each other in 1987. I was vice-president of one of the Nationalist organizations. I was traveling in a bus at that time and was forcibly abducted, arrested, and tortured. That is when Mother, Father, and Munawar also became active in the Sindhi Nationalist Movement led by Qadir Magsi who had gone underground and continued to work.

I left active politics in 1988 and resumed my normal life, but Father, Mother, and Munawar continued to work actively for the movement. Qadir Magsi was arrested on September 30th and all of Sindh erupted in protest. My parents continued to lead that movement. After a while that movement was also splintered. That was when Munawar went underground and continued to work for the movement. My younger cousin, Karim, was in prison for five years. It became impossible for Munawar to work for the movement without endangering his life and, in 1993, he was forced into exile. Mother was very attached to Munawar, and she pined to see him all the time. This separation was unbearable for her, and her health crumbled under the strain.

Mother loved me, my wife, my son, and my two daughters beyond measure. My son was her favorite grandchild, perhaps because he was her first grandchild. When my son Assad secured 88 percent marks in ninth standard, she had the mark sheet laminated and proudly kept with her. My son is the look-alike of his uncle Munawar too. When Assad appeared for his matriculation examination, she prayed for his success with good grades. Alas! The result came on the very same day that she left this world.

Chapter 29: Remembering My Mother by Anwar

She was very particular about cleanliness, and she would wash clothes herself and fold them in the manner that did not require any further pressing. She was very considerate to domestic workers and would always extend a helping hand to complete their assigned chores.

She fell seriously ill about six months before her departure. We took her to the doctors, and they diagnosed it as cancer. I took leave from my work under the circumstances and served my mother. I was thus afforded a unique opportunity to redeem my debt to her to some extent, though I shall always remain indebted to her for her love and affection that I received in abundance. Water would collect in her abdomen. Even in such a grim situation, we got good news: My parents were invited to interview for a visa to travel to the United States to visit Munawar. He was very attached to his mother, too, and he made it his duty to inquire about her heath daily. I accompanied them to the embassy in Islamabad for that purpose. I had many friends at Islamabad who were attached to the hospital, and they all revered her as their own mother. During tests that were conducted, she had to pass through a lot of painful procedures. I nursed her in the hospital, and she continued to shower her blessings. Her blessings brought tears to my eyes. I had to control myself lest she might be disturbed. Munawar's coworker, Hamira Rehman, came from Canada to visit her. Doctors were in a difficult position. Though we all knew that her days were numbered, they had to certify her fit to travel to the United States. These doctors were indebted to her from their student days, having been fed by her as their own mother would, so they did certify her as "fit" to travel. In all this Dr. Ismail Memon stood with us like a rock. Our stay at Islamabad was also arranged by my dear friends.

With the grace of God, Mother got a visa to visit the United States to see her beloved son at last. We flew to Karachi the next day and then reached Hyderabad by taxi. It appeared in this time before she departed for the United States that the happiness brought by the thought of seeing Munawar had absolved her of all her pain. Her son had settled beyond seven seas and built his nest there. She eagerly awaited the moment she would be able to fulfill her long cherished desire. Her determination was overwhelming indeed! She could stare death in face and challenge it!

We all went to the Karachi airport to see them off. My father, who had weathered nearly half century with my mother, was now going with her at this critical time. My father was himself not very educated, but he had a great respect for learning and was an ardent student of Shah Latif, the soul of Sindh. We gave him many instructions about how to move at the airport, but he appeared to be unmindful of all our instructions; rather, he had self-confidence that, with the grace of God, they would not face any difficulty.

I inquired of Munawar after 24 hours about their status, and he confirmed that Father and Mother had reached his house and that they were comfortable. After some days he conveyed to me the news that our parents had even received a Green Card. While she was in United States, she instructed Munawar to keep up his work for his motherland Sindh to restore its past glory.

Munawar called on May 29th to say that he was accompanying Mother and Father to Dubai. We reached Karachi airport to receive them on June 1st. It took them some time to come out of the airport; then after nearly two hours, I saw an old lady wearing a cap and a coat emerging in a wheelchair. I told Assad and Sabeeh that she was our Old Mother. Father came out pushing her wheelchair. I ran to touch their

Chapter 29: Remembering My Mother by Anwar

feet, and the tears would not stop pouring from my eyes. In explaining the reason for the delay, Father said that one of their bags had not arrived from Dubai. They had to complete the necessary formalities. We moved toward Hyderabad. Mother had lost quite a lot of weight and appeared to be a mere skeleton. She asked for some water but could not drink it.

As she was getting out of the car at their Hyderabad residence, she removed gold rings from her fingers and said that now they were for her grandson, Assad, before handing them to my wife. I kept up conversation on the way, so that she did not lapse into sleep and kept inquiring about Munawar and the United States. She was quite enthusiastic to speak about Munawar. She never wore new clothes on occasion of Eid after Munawar had left.

Whenever this song would play on the radio, she would shed copious tears remembering her son!

> *"Beloved is at every place in every gathering*
> *I keenly felt your absence*
> *I cherished your memories in the heart*
> *But your absence is keenly felt"*

We would switch off the radio or change the TV channel immediately.

When she became very weak, she would ask for support to get up. We would tell her to rest completely, but she would retort by saying when guests come to inquire about her health, it did not absolve her from her to meet and greet them. This was our social tradition, and she refused to abandon it.

Mother appeared to be improving after some time, but it was a deceptive sign. In spite of her weakness, she would indulge her grandchildren and play cards with them. They would urge her to sing songs, and sometimes they would ask her to sing her favorite lullaby, and she would never fail to enchant them.

She was always concerned about Assad's education. She would always recommend Munawar to look after the future of Assad. She wanted him to be educated in a foreign country for higher education, and that duty was assigned to Munawar.

She called all my three children the day before her departure. She loved them with all her heart, and she showered her blessings on them. She requested Assad to connect her to Munawar by phone, but he could not be contacted. Eventually, when Munawar called her, she could not respond. Munawar pitifully kept asking our mother to say something, as he was desperate to hear her voice, but all he got from our side was a deep silence! She simply held the hand on her grandson, and we all started crying. It was 10:30 a.m. on Friday, June 27, 2008 when Munawar disconnected his phone....

About The Author

Chacha Muhammad Ali Laghari loved Sindh; and as a humanitarian he always struggled for the rights of Sindh from various platforms.

Chacha Muhammad Ali Laghari's love for Latif and his unique understanding and explanation of Latif's philosophy was also apparent in his recital of Latif's poetry in his speeches.

Chacha Muhammad Ali Laghari was the center of attention in all gatherings, and was very friendly with people of all ages.

Chacha Muhammad Ali Laghari never betrayed anyone's trust in his life.

May Gold bless him with health and long life so he can serve the oppressed people of Sindh.

By: 'Professor Liaqat Aziz'

Fatima of Sindh

Chacha Mohammed Ali Laghari transitioned into eternal peace on September 1, 2016.

Chacha Mohammed Ali Laghari
August 1, 1940 - September 1, 2016

www.ingramcontent.com/pod-product-compliance
Lightning Source LLC
Chambersburg PA
CBHW071608170426
43196CB00034B/2242